RESEARCH ON THE INTERNET

Videocassette Program

Teaching Notes with Worksheets and Answer Keys

HOLT, RINEHART AND WINSTON
Harcourt Brace & Company
Austin • New York • Orlando • Atlanta • San Francisco • Boston • Dallas • Toronto • London

Staff Credits

Associate Director: Mescal K. Evler
Project Editors: Amy Strong, Michael L. Smith
Technology Project Editor: Lydia Doty
Copyediting Supervisor: Michael Neibergall
Copyeditors: Barbara Sutherland, Katherine E. Hoyt, Joel Bourgeois, Roger Boylan, Carrie Laing Pickett
Media Production Coordinator: Belinda Barboza
Design: Joe Melomo, Design Manager; Neel Heisel, Designer
Cover Illustration: Greg Geisler
Composition: Debra Schorn
Permissions: Carrie Jones

Acknowledgments

For permission to use copyrighted material in the Videocassette, grateful acknowledgment is given to the following sources:

The Board of Trustees of the University of Illinois, on behalf of its National Center for Supercomputing Applications: NSFNet Images from *Visualization Study of the NSFNET* by Donna Cox and Robert Patterson, July 14, 1992, Online, World Wide Web, February 6, 1997. Copyright © 1992 by National Center for Supercomputing Applications. Available http://www.ncsa.uiuc.edu/scms/DigLib/stills.

Britannica Online, Version 97.1.1: "Gypsy" from *Britannica Online, Version 97.1.1,* Online, World Wide Web, February 6, 1997. Copyright © 1997 by Encyclopædia Britannica, Inc. Available http://www.eb.com:180/eb.html.

Embassy of Spain, Education Office: *Welcome to "Sí, Spain"/Bienvenido a "Sí, España,"* Online, World Wide Web, February 6, 1997. Available http://www.docuweb.ca/SiSpain/index.html.

Infoseek Corporation: Search results from "Foreign Countries" from *Infoseek,* February 7, 1997, Online, World Wide Web. Copyright © 1995–1997 by Infoseek Corporation. All rights reserved. Infoseek, Ultrasmart, ¡Seek, Quickseek, Imageseek, Ultrashop, "proof of intelligent life on the net," and the Infoseek logo are trademarks of Infoseek Corporation which may be registered in certain jurisdictions. Other trademarks shown are trademarks of their respective owners. Available http://www.infoseek.com.

Netscape Communications Corporation: Netscape Navigator interface. Copyright © 1997 by Netscape Communications Corporation. All rights reserved. This page may not be reprinted or copied without the express written permission of Netscape. Netscape is a trademark of Netscape Communications Corporation, which is registered in the United States and other countries. Available http://home.netscape.com/.

The Patrin: "*The Patrin* URL Pointer," "Index to *The Patrin,*" "A Brief History of the Roma," "Roma in Culture and the Arts," and "Further Reading" from *The Patrin,* January 29, 1997, Online, World Wide Web, February 6, 1997. Copyright © 1996–1997 by The Patrin. Available http://www.geocities.com/Paris/5121/patrin.htm.

Rebecca Tracy: "Annotated List of References" from *Romani Rights Web,* September 17, 1995, Online, February 6, 1997. Copyright © 1995–1996 by Rebecca Tracy. Available http://hamp.hampshire.edu/~ratS88/romani/.

University of Michigan Documents Center: "Army Area Handbook" and "Foreign Governments: Country Background" from *University of Michigan Documents Center,* January 26, 1997, Online, World Wide Web, February 6, 1997. Copyright © 1997 by the University of Michigan. Available http://www.lib.umich.edu/libhome/Documents.center/forcount.html.

YAHOO!: Search for "Sí, Spain" from *Yahoo!,* February 7, 1997, Online, World Wide Web. Text and artwork copyright © 1996 by YAHOO!, Inc. All rights reserved. YAHOO! and the YAHOO! logo are trademarks of YAHOO!, Inc. Available http://www.yahoo.com.

Printed in the United States of America

ISBN 0-03-052244-7

4 5 179 01

Contents

NOTE TO THE TEACHER: USING THE *RESEARCH ON THE INTERNET VIDEOCASSETTE PROGRAM*

Welcome to the world of the Internet! The ***Research on the Internet Videocassette Program*** is an introduction to the use of the Internet as a tool for student research. If you have little or no experience using the Internet, the videotape will be useful for you as well as for your students. In the *Teaching Notes* you will find more in-depth information and hands-on activities for your students. Even if you are already a frequent World Wide Web visitor, this program will help you guide your students through the more challenging phases of the research process—source evaluation and documentation.

By following the presentation guidelines below, you can provide your students with the background and skills they need to conduct thoughtful and productive research online. In particular, the *Research on the Internet* program will enable your students to

- develop a concept of the Internet and the World Wide Web
- understand key vocabulary associated with the Internet
- use a Web browser
- use Web search engines and browsable directories to find information sources
- evaluate information found in Web sites
- document Web sites cited in research papers

Assessing Students' Knowledge and Skills

Before showing the videotape to your students, take inventory of their Internet knowledge and skills. While some of your students may already be proficient "Web surfers," it's likely that all will benefit from instruction on advanced search and evaluation techniques. The Activity 1: K-W-L-W-L Teaching Guide and its accompanying worksheet (pages 5 and 6) will allow you to assess your students' current level of expertise in using the World Wide Web as a research tool.

Viewing the Videotape

After students complete columns 1 and 2 of the Activity 1 worksheet, show the videotape. The tape is divided into four sections, separated by title screens. Pause the tape each time a new title screen appears, and take a few minutes to lead a quick review of the section students have just seen. Then, ask students to write responses to the section in columns 3 and 4 of the worksheet. For the reviews, draw on the *Teaching Notes* as needed; the sections are summarized on pages 2 and 3. Note that the tape is just over twenty-three minutes long; during a single class period, you should be able to show the tape, conduct reviews, and have students complete columns 1 to 4 of the worksheet.

Reassessing Student Knowledge

Collect and evaluate students' worksheets; then, selectively teach from the remainder of the *Teaching Notes,* based on what students still need or want to learn.

Providing Further Instruction and Activities

After assessing students' comfort level with the Internet and the World Wide Web, turn to the sections of the book covering the Internet research skills that your students need to develop. By reading the background information, providing students with informational handouts, and following the lesson plans provided, you will be ready to lead your students in hands-on Internet research activities. A description of the resources provided in the *Teaching Notes* appears on page 4.

OVERVIEW OF THE VIDEOTAPE

This videotape introduces students to the fundamentals of conducting research on the Internet through the use of three likable characters and a real-world situation. The videotape begins with an overview of the Internet, focusing on its most popular interface, the World Wide Web. The viewer then learns the features and functions of a Web browser. Next, the characters in the video demonstrate the use of search engines and directories to find and narrow their research topics. Finally, the viewer learns how to evaluate information sources found on the Web.

The Key Vocabulary boxes contain terms that are introduced in each section of the videotape. Definitions of Key Vocabulary terms appear in the Glossary, which may be reproduced for student use.

Scenario

The story that serves as a vehicle for the instructional content of the video revolves around two students. Vanessa Mendoza is a bright and accomplished high school junior who has had very little experience doing research on the World Wide Web. In her efforts to get up to speed in this area, she has enlisted the aid of Tony Hillman, who is already proficient at searching for information on the Web. They work with a teacher, Mrs. Turner, who helps them develop the skills they need to evaluate Web information sources. As the characters interact to solve real-world research problems, the following topics are addressed.

Key Topics Covered

PART ONE: GETTING YOUR WEB FEET WET
An Introduction to the Internet and the World Wide Web

The beginning of the video finds Tony waiting for Vanessa in the school media center. As he waits, he fills the viewers in on some basic Internet background information. Specifically, this section of the videotape provides viewers with

- a brief overview of the Internet
- an overview of the World Wide Web
- an explanation of the relationship of the Web to the Internet

KEY VOCABULARY:
Internet
World Wide Web

PART TWO: READ ANY GOOD WEB PAGES LATELY?
Getting Started on the World Wide Web

In this section, students will be introduced to the Web browser, the doorway to the vast information resources on the World Wide Web. The video will feature the browser Netscape, but the general concepts will apply to any browser—Netscape, Internet Explorer, Mosaic, and so on.

KEY VOCABULARY:
cyberspace
URL
Web browser
Web site

PART THREE: SEARCH PARTY

Searching for Information on the World Wide Web

In this segment, Vanessa uses the World Wide Web to find and narrow a subject for her research assignment, which is to write a report on some aspect of a world culture. As Tony helps Vanessa use the Web to refine her subject, the two students will demonstrate the use of

- keyword search engines, such as Infoseek
- browsable directories, such as Yahoo

This section illustrates the opportunities for critical thinking that using the Web provides. Viewers learn that searching is not a passive activity conducted by the computer; on the contrary, the user needs to interact with the search engine to get successful search results. Vanessa gradually learns to narrow her searches in order to get better results from the search engine; by doing so, she also successfully narrows her subject to a workable research paper topic.

KEY VOCABULARY:
search engine
results
hyperlink
directory

PART FOUR: WHO SAYS SO, ANYWAY?

Evaluating Sources on the World Wide Web

The final segment of the video provides viewers with tools for evaluating and documenting sources. Having selected a topic and located several different sites related to that topic, Vanessa's challenge is to decide which of these sites will be useful for further research and which will not be. Mrs. Turner helps the two students discover the five basic criteria for evaluating Web sites. Tony and Vanessa use these criteria to evaluate Vanessa's sources, and they conclude that the standards used to evaluate Web sources are basically the same as those that apply to print materials.

Overview of the Teaching Notes

The parts of the *Teaching Notes* correspond to the four major parts of the videocassette. Each part in the *Teaching Notes,* however, contains more in-depth information and covers additional topics. Much of the information in these sections appears on reproducible pages that you may elect to hand out to your students. These pages fall into two categories:

- **Internet Basics.** These handouts provide basic background information on the Internet and the World Wide Web. If your students want or need to develop an understanding of basic Internet concepts, these handouts will be helpful.
- **Web Research Essentials.** These handouts provide information that your students will need in order to understand the basic concepts and skills involved with using the Web for research.

In addition to these informational handouts, the *Teaching Notes* provide activities that your students can use to develop Internet research skills. Each activity consists of a Teaching Guide page and a Worksheet, most of which your students can use to carry out real research projects on the Web.

At the end of the *Teaching Notes,* you will find the following resources.

- **Appendix A: Documenting World Wide Web Sources.** This section includes detailed information for the teacher, quick-reference handouts, and a documentation information log for students.
- **Appendix B: World Wide Web Resources.** This section provides an interdisciplinary, annotated listing of useful information sources on the World Wide Web.
- **Glossary: Internet and World Wide Web Terms.** The glossary provides definitions of key terms that appear in the videotape and of other important Internet-related terms.
- **Answer Keys.** The Answer Keys provide answers to worksheet questions or suggestions for evaluating responses.

This activity is an adaptation of the traditional K-W-L activity, in which students use a chart with three headings—"What I Know," "What I Want to Know," and "What I Learned"—to show their prior knowledge, their goals, and, finally, their reflections on knowledge or skills gained from an instructional unit. This activity takes the traditional K-W-L activity two steps further.

Objectives

- Students actively view and take notes on *Research on the Internet.*
- Students analyze their viewing to identify information that provides adequate responses to their K-W-L questions.
- Students analyze their viewing to identify K-W-L questions that still need to be addressed.
- Students synthesize what they knew before viewing with what they learned in viewing to develop additional questions.

Presentation

Before Viewing. Prepare students for the previewing activity by asking them how they think the World Wide Web might be used in the research process. For example, for which stages of research might the Web be most useful? What special problems might be involved in using the Web? Distribute the K-W-L-W-L chart to individual or paired students. Have the students complete column 1 by coming up with a general list of what they already know about using the World Wide Web in the research process. Then, ask them to come up with at least three things they would like to learn about using the Web in research and to enter those goals in column 2.

Viewing. After students complete columns 1 and 2 of the worksheet, show the videotape. The tape is divided into four sections, separated by title screens. Pause the tape each time a new title screen appears, and take a few minutes to lead a quick review of the section students have just seen. Then, ask students to write responses to the section in columns 3 and 4 of the worksheet. (Explain that in column 4, they may note questions from column 2 that the section did not answer, or new questions that they thought of as they watched the section.) For the reviews, draw on the *Teaching Notes* as needed; the sections are summarized on pages 2 and 3. Note that the tape is just over twenty-three minutes long; during a single class period, you should be able to show the tape, conduct reviews, and have students complete columns 1 to 4 of the worksheet.

After Viewing. Collect the worksheets and proceed with the directions below.

Assessing Students' Knowledge and Skills

As you sort through the charts, pay particular attention to columns 1 and 4, and create different stacks—one for students who want to know more about the Internet and the World Wide Web in general, one for students who are comfortable with the basics but need to know more about using search engines, and one for students who understand search engines but want to know more about evaluating sources. By grouping the charts into these general skill areas, you will be able to use activities in this booklet that meet each student's needs.

Cooperative Learning

You may want to place the students represented in each stack into cooperative groups. If so, you can introduce a mix of ability levels into each group based on students' responses in the first column. For example, students who demonstrated a high level of proficiency with the Web but who indicated that they wanted to know more about evaluation could be grouped with students who indicated a lower comfort level with Web basics.

Evaluation

After completing one or more activities provided in this booklet, have students reflect on their learning by filling out column 5 of the K-W-L-W-L chart.

NAME ______________ CLASS ______________ DATE ______________

ACTIVITY 1 K-W-L-W-L

Worksheet

1 What I Know	2 What I Want to Know	3 What I Learned: Postviewing	4 What I Want to Know: Postviewing	5 What I Learned
About the Internet and the World Wide Web				
About Web Browsers and Search Engines				
About Evaluating Web Sites				

PART ONE: GETTING YOUR WEB FEET WET

An Introduction to the Internet and the World Wide Web

This section provides background information on the Internet and the World Wide Web. Your students don't need to have all of the information to begin using the Web, but you may want to share it with them to be sure that they have a solid conceptual foundation for their Internet explorations. The information is provided in the following handouts:

Along with these handouts, the section also contains essential information for students who will be doing research on the Web. This information appears in the following handout:

In addition, important Internet safety information specifically for teachers and school computer administrators is provided below.

Safety Alert: Protecting Students from Inappropriate Parts of the Internet

You've most likely heard about some of the potential dangers on the fringes of the Internet—chat rooms devoted to discussions of "mature" topics, "adults-only" Usenet newsgroups, Web sites containing objectionable language and images—and you're probably concerned about protecting your students from them. You're not alone. Because many other educators and parents share your concern, software companies have developed computer programs, called *filtering* or *blocking* applications, to allow young people to use the Internet safely and appropriately. These programs can enable you to

- prevent students from sending out personal information, such as their home phone numbers or addresses
- restrict student access to prohibited Usenet newsgroups
- monitor the keywords that students use to search for information, and block them from sending out keywords that might take them to objectionable sites
- deny student access to any of a large number of "off-limits" Internet sites that the program's creators and users have judged to be inappropriate for young people

To protect your students and avoid potential problems, make sure your school has blocking software before you assign Internet activities. You may also want to take steps like the ones below to discourage students from *intentionally* accessing inappropriate materials.

1. Provide your students with written conduct rules stating what kinds of uses of the Internet are acceptable at your site, and what kinds are not.
2. Ask students to agree to the rules before they are given Internet privileges.
3. Make it clear that their Internet privileges will be revoked if they violate the rules.

Of course, you shouldn't depend completely on software or rules. The best way for you to ensure that your students use the Internet appropriately at school is to always monitor their Internet activity and to never permit them to access the Internet unsupervised.

INTERNET BASICS ⟨1⟩ The Internet and the World Wide Web

If the personal computers in a school computer lab are connected to one another with cables so that they can transfer files (documents, images, sounds, and programs) to each other, they form what is called a *network.* If a longer cable is added between the lab and a classroom that also has computers, the network becomes bigger and more useful, because files can then be shared between any of the lab computers and any of the computers in the classroom. To go a step further, existing telephone lines can be used to connect the school network to a network of more powerful computers at a nearby university, allowing students at the school to use the school's computers to exchange files not only with the university but also with any other computers or networks that can be reached from the university, including those in other cities, states, or countries.

The Internet

Today, computers around the world are connected in this way, and the resulting global "network of networks" is collectively referred to as *the Internet.* The Internet uses some of the same equipment developed to make our telephone networks. In fact, it's common for people to connect to the Internet over the telephone lines they also use to call their neighbors—though better, faster (and more expensive) lines are now available.

When people first started to share files between computers on the Internet, they had to agree on common signals (or *protocols*) to use so that the computers could know what to expect from each other, and what to do with files once they were transferred. The idea was for the computers to communicate this "housekeeping" information to each other behind the scenes, without people ever needing to worry about it. Early on, people agreed on protocols to use for sending text, and e-mail was born. Over the years, they agreed on more protocols for doing such things as sending pictures, transferring programs, and setting up online bulletin boards. Many of the older protocols are still around today, and computers can use several sets of them at once.

The World Wide Web

One of the newest protocols allows computers to send, receive, and display integrated *multimedia* (styled text, sound, video, animation, programs, and interactive "broadcasts" of all kinds). It's called *HTTP* (Hypertext Transfer Protocol), and it's the basis for what is commonly called the World Wide Web. Programs that are designed to work mainly with HTTP are called *Web browsers.* Some Web browsers are also capable of working with other protocols, many of which remain in use. The list below shows what these other protocols are still used for.

- E-mail: Send and receive electronic messages
- Usenet: Read and post messages to newsgroups (online discussion forums)
- Telnet: Log on to remote computers, using your computer as a terminal (text only)
- Gopher: Browse subject-oriented menus to find files
- File Transfer Protocol (FTP): Transfer files (mostly used for large files)

People often assume that the World Wide Web *is* the Internet. As we've just shown, though, it's a *part* of the Internet—the part that uses HTTP. However, it's the first place that many people put files for others to access, and the first place that many look for information. In fact, if you're planning on using the Internet to conduct research, the Web is the part of it that you are likely to visit most.

If you've ever mailed packages, and you can visualize how they made their way through the mail from you to the people you sent them to, you can also visualize how information moves around on the Internet.

To mail a set of small packages to the same destination, you address them and drop them in a mailbox that holds a bunch of other letters and packages. The Postal Service sorts and delivers them from there. The packages may be carried to a substation by a postal worker on foot, then transferred by truck to a bigger substation, and then, perhaps, loaded onto a plane. Along the way they get mixed in with more and more mail, until, when they get close to the destination, the are sorted into smaller groups again. Your packages then move from the plane back to a truck, and then to another postal worker on foot, who finally delivers them.

How Messages Travel on the Internet

On the Internet, messages sent by your computer travel in units called *packets,* mixed with packets from other computers, and they move over telephone lines and cables to *routers* (computers acting as delivery substations) that decide where to send them next, until they reach their destinations. Each step, from one router to the next, is called a *hop.* If a message reaches one of the Internet's "backbone" routes (the fast, high-capacity lines between big cities), its next hop can be quite large, as Figure 1-1 shows.

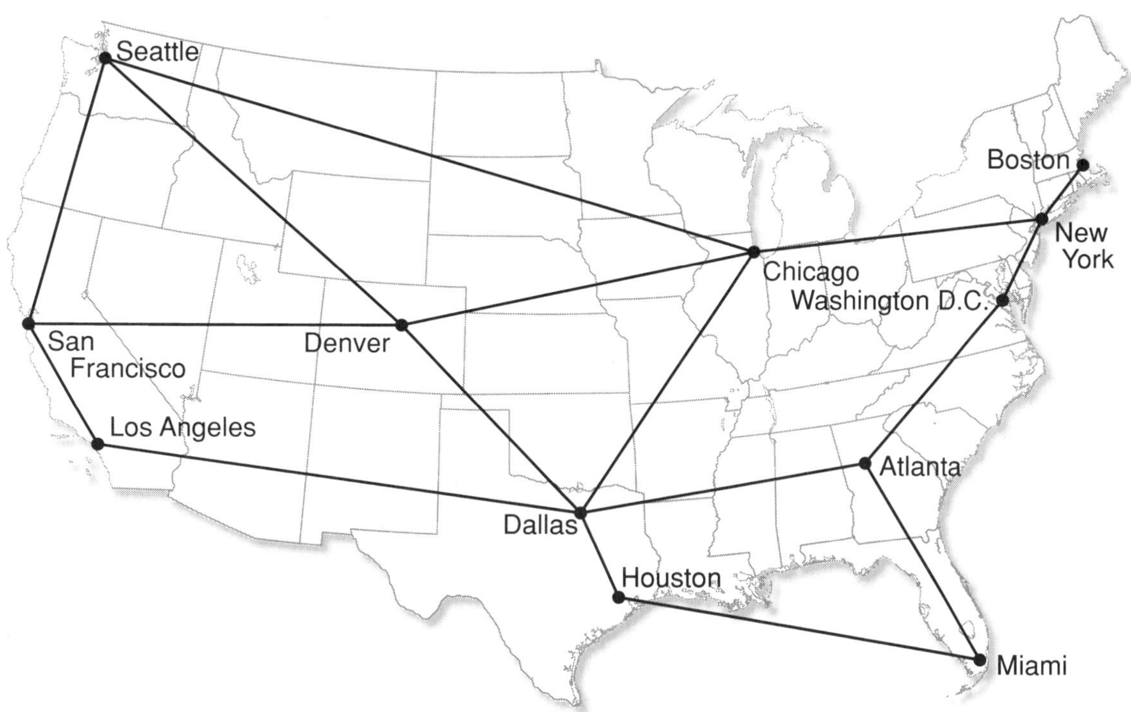

Figure 1-1: Some of the major routes on the Internet

A message traveling from Los Angeles along one of the backbone routes might "hop" to Dallas, then to Chicago, then to New York, and then to Boston. It could also take a different path, say: San Francisco, Denver, Chicago, New York, Boston. Or it might use a route not shown here. Routers along the way decide which path is best.

WEB RESEARCH ESSENTIALS 1
Reading an Internet Address

Each file on the Internet has a unique address, called a Uniform Resource Locator or URL. To evaluate a source you find on the Internet, it helps to understand something about the parts that make up a URL. The illustration below, of the URL for the Internal Revenue Service's "Forms and Publications" Web page, shows what each part is called.

protocol code | path

http://www.irs.ustreas.gov/prod/forms_pubs/index.html

hostname | filename

The *.html* (for *Hypertext Markup Language*) extension on the filename tells you that the file is a Web page. The protocol code (*http://*, for *Hypertext Transfer Protocol*) tells you that the file is stored on a Web server (an Internet computer that stores and sends Web pages). The hostname is made up of several components separated by periods or "dots." The first component, *www,* is the label the IRS has given to its Web server. Web servers are commonly labeled *www,* for *World Wide Web.* (In contrast, the IRS has a server, labeled *ftp,* that it uses as its FTP server. Its complete hostname is *ftp.irs.ustreas.gov.*)

The other components of the hostname (irs, ustreas, gov) are called domains. If you read through the hostname backward (from right to left, the way Internet computers would decipher it), you will find that each domain you run into contains all of the ones before it.

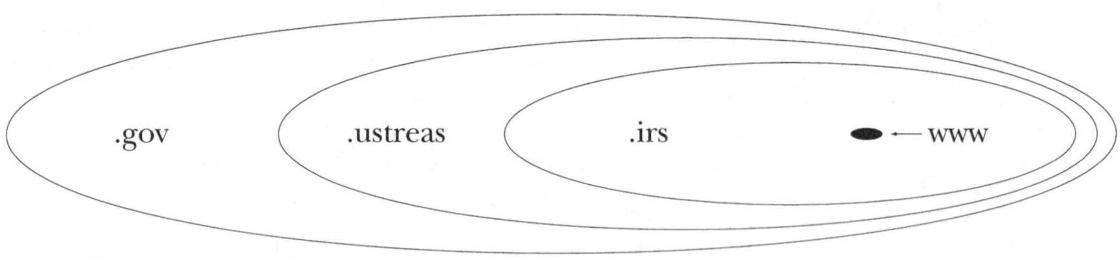

So, in the example hostname, *gov* is the domain that contains all of the servers of the U.S. government, *ustreas* is the domain that contains all of the servers of the U.S. Treasury Department (one part of the government), and *irs* is the domain that contains all of the servers of the Internal Revenue Service (one part of the Treasury Department). The remaining component, *www,* is the label the IRS has given to its Web server.

The *gov* domain is one of several "top-level" U.S. domains. Others include

- **edu** educational and research sites (colleges, schools, and some museums)
- **com** commercial sites (businesses; groups that don't fit in other categories)
- **mil** military (U.S.) sites (many not directly related to the armed services)
- **org** organizations (usually nonprofit)
- **net** network service providers (organizations that offer Internet services)

Hostnames for non-U.S. sites often use different abbreviations, and usually end in a two-letter country code. For example, the hostname for Yahoo's U.S. site is *www.yahoo.com,* but the name for its Japanese site is *www.yahoo.co.jp.* Outside the U.S., *co* is used instead of *com, or* instead of *org,* and *ac* (academic) instead of *edu.* Some hostnames end in *us,* the two-letter code for the United States; they may also contain a two-letter state code. For example, the hostname for a server maintained by the El Paso (Texas) Independent School District is *www.elpaso.k12.tx.us.* In place of *edu,* many U.S. elementary and secondary schools use the domain *k12,* plus a state code, plus *us.*

PART TWO: READ ANY GOOD WEB PAGES LATELY?

Getting Started on the World Wide Web

This section provides you with a brief summary of key concepts relating to the World Wide Web, and a short explanation of what your students can expect when they begin to "Web surf." For students who are specifically preparing for research on the Web, this section also contains essential information on Web browser software and on troubleshooting browser problems. This information is provided in the following handouts:

- Web Research Essentials 2: Parts of a Browser and How to Use Them (page 13)
- Web Research Essentials 3: Troubleshooting Potential Problems (page 14)

If you would prefer to lead students in a guided activity that presents the same information as the Web Research Essentials 2 handout, use the Teaching Guide on page 15, and provide students with the following worksheet:

Activity 2: Using a Browser (Worksheet, page 16)

If your students haven't explored the Web much and they're wondering how it might be useful, the list of features below might help you to sell them on it.

- **Offers access to a huge variety of information.** Because the Web contains literally millions of documents, you can find information on almost any subject.
- **Searchable.** You can use online search tools to find, among all of those millions of Web documents, only the documents that include keywords you provide.
- **Multimedia-enriched.** Web documents can contain pictures, sounds, animation, and videos, and the Web can incorporate newer technologies as they spring up.
- **Easy to use.** If you know how to point and click with a mouse, you can use the Web. You don't need to be a computer expert or to learn arcane commands.
- **Links together related resources.** One Web document may link to a hundred other related ones, and you can access them all with the click of a mouse button.
- **Open to everybody.** Anyone can publish a document on the Web.

However, the best way to convince students that the Web can be a useful tool is to get them started on it. The Web is so user-friendly that little preparation is needed to start "surfing" on it right away. The following paragraphs describe what your students can expect when they first use the Web.

Hyperlinks

When students sit down to explore the Web for the first time, they normally start either at a page the browser automatically loads at startup, or they type in addresses for *Web sites* that they'd like to go to. From there, they can *browse* without ever typing in an address, by following *hyperlinks.* A hyperlink is a "hot spot" on a page that they can point to and click on with a mouse. Clicking on one usually causes a browser to display a different page.

Words that are hyperlinks are called *hypertext*; your students will usually be able to identify hypertext because it is most often underlined and in a different, brighter color than the other words on the page. Images in a page may also act as hyperlinks; however, not all images in a document will be hyperlinks, and not all differently colored words will be hypertext. When the cursor falls on a word or image that is a hyperlink, the cursor arrow will change; in Netscape, for example, the arrow changes to a pointing hand. When your students click on a "hot" hyperlink with this pointing hand, they might access a different page.

Hyperlinks are encoded into a document using a formatting language called *HTML* (Hypertext Markup Language). HTML codes tell a browser how the text, images, links, and other parts of a page should be styled and arranged. For example, the code <B></B> is used to mark all terms that will appear in boldface. A browser reads a coded word like this: <B>boldface</B>, but displays it like this: **boldface.** The term *Web page* is used to refer to any HTML file that is stored on a computer that can be accessed over the Internet.

Clients and Servers

When a computer works with HTML files over the Internet, it takes one of two roles. It either acts as a client, or it acts as a server. Roughly speaking, Web servers store and send files to clients that request and display them. When students use personal computers to browse the Web, they are using them as clients. It's similar to cable television: TV sets are clients, and cable companies are servers. Cable TV viewers press buttons on remote controls to "request" channels offered by cable companies; your students will click on hyperlinks to request Web pages from Web servers.

While servers are typically fast computers that can store many files, the only real difference is this: servers are computers that run server software, and clients are computers that run client software. Anyone can put server software on a personal computer and connect it to the Internet to turn it into an Internet server. In fact, although personal computer servers are slower than "real" servers, there are many of them on the Internet. Students may access them without noticing a difference. Figure 2-1 illustrates what happens when a student clicks on a hyperlink or types in a URL to request an HTML file from a Web server.

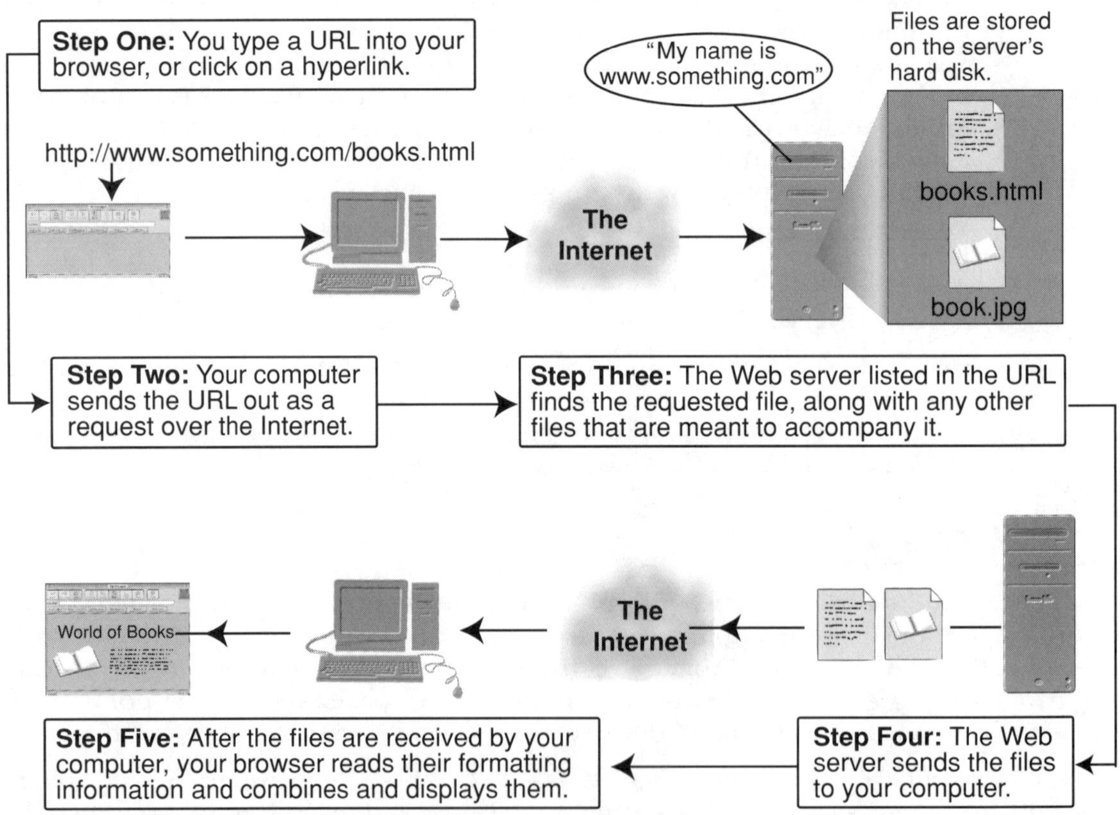

Figure 2-1: What happens after you type in a URL or click on a hyperlink

Servers, like most computers, store files in directories on hard disks. A *Web site* is a group of Web pages connected by hyperlinks and stored in one set of directories on a server. Every Web site has a *home page*—a starting point from which, using a browser, you can follow links to other pages available at the site.

WEB RESEARCH ESSENTIALS 2

Parts of a Web Browser and How to Use Them

Figure 2-2 shows images of two typical browsers: Netscape's Navigator and Microsoft's Internet Explorer. (These simplified, black-and-white images are proportioned to fit this page. A browser on a computer monitor will look much different.) Following the images are short explanations of what the various parts of the browsers show or do.

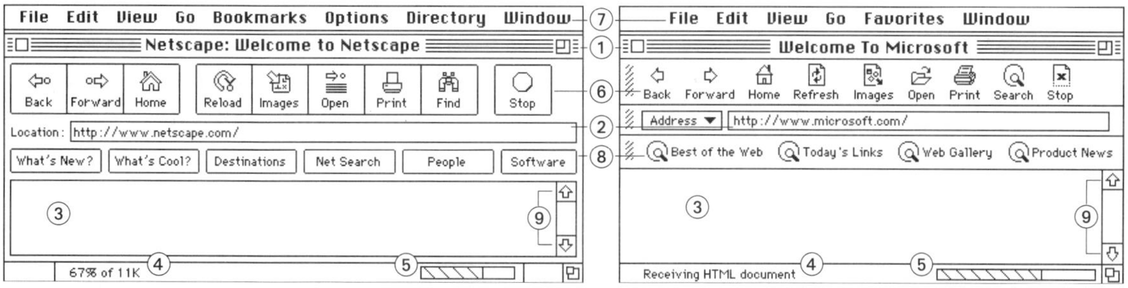

Figure 2-2: Netscape Navigator 3.0 (left) and Microsoft Internet Explorer 3.0 (right)

1. **Title Bar.** Shows the title of the page currently displayed.
2. **Location Window.** Shows the URL of the page currently displayed. One of two places where you can type in URLs you wish to access.
3. **Main Window.** Displays the Web page at the URL in the Location Window
4. **Status Line.** Shows the URL for any hyperlink to which the cursor is pointing. It gives other information when you are connecting to a server. As you view a page, it also tells how much of the page has loaded and how fast it is loading.
5. **Progress Bar.** Graphically represents how much of a total page has loaded.
6. **Toolbar Buttons.** Click on these to activate some of the most commonly used navigation commands. Most browsers have these buttons above the location window.
   Back. Go back to the page you loaded before the one currently displayed.
   Forward. Move ahead again through any pages that you got to using **Back.**
   Home. Go back to the page your browser is set to display when it starts up.
   Reload/Refresh. Cause the current page to be reloaded.
   Images. Load images in the current page, if your browser is not set for auto loading.
   Open. Call up a box where you can type in a URL for a page you wish to view.
   Print. Print the page currently displayed in your browser's main window.
   Find/Search. Search for terms within the page currently displayed.
   Stop. Interrupt loading of the page currently displayed.
7. **Menus.** Select a variety of commands from these. Many menu commands mirror the functions of toolbar buttons. Here's information on some menu commands for which there are no buttons.
   File. Select **Save as** to save Web pages to your computer's hard disk.
   Bookmarks/Favorites. Use a menu command to mark pages you may want to go back to. To view marked pages, select them from here instead of retyping their URLs.
8. **Directory Buttons.** Click on these to get to predetermined Web pages. These may help when you first use the Web. To create more space for Web pages, though, you can choose the option of "hiding" these buttons.
9. **Scrollbar** and **Scroll Buttons.** Use these to move up and down through pages.

WEB RESEARCH ESSENTIALS 3

Troubleshooting Potential Problems

With any browser, you may sometimes run into difficulties accessing the Web. This page lists some common access problems, along with explanations of how to deal with them.

Pages appear too slowly. The main factor affecting the speed at which pages appear on your screen is the nature of your computer's Internet connection. Modems severely limit how quickly pages get to you. Computers with "dedicated" non-modem connections may receive pages ten times as quickly. A graphics-heavy Web page may cause a modem to reach its limit. If your connection is modem-based, be patient, and expect some waiting. If you don't need to see the images on a page, adjust your browser settings so that the images do not automatically load with the text.

Another major factor is the nature of the server from which you're trying to get Web pages. If it's a large, powerful computer with a high-speed connection, it will seem to send pages as fast as your computer can handle them. A smaller server with a slower connection won't be able to send pages as quickly. No matter how fast your own connection is, you'll need to wait to get pages from one of these slower servers.

Only part of a page appears. Servers sometimes seem to stall and "forget" to finish loading pages you've started to see. When this happens, click your browser's **Stop** button, and then click **Reload.** If this doesn't fix the problem, chances are that the server is just overloaded, and you're better off trying again later.

An error message appears on the screen. Although you may see a variety of error messages, most of them are caused by the same few problems:

1. You've typed in an incorrect URL. If even one letter is wrong in the hostname portion of a URL, the page will not load. Carefully check the URLs you type in.
2. You've typed in what was once a correct URL, but the server or file it refers to has since been removed or renamed. Try a keyword search to find the updated URL.
3. Your Internet connection has gone down, or you were not connected when you opened your browser. Restarting your computer can sometimes fix this problem.
4. You've reached the server listed in the URL, but it's too busy (overloaded with requests) or has been temporarily shut down. Take a break and try it again later.

Here's the specific wording of some common error messages you're likely to see:

Unable to locate the server. The server does not have a DNS entry. Check the server name in the URL and try again.	See Reasons 1, 2, and 3. If you get this message with every URL, see Reason 3.
Network connection refused by the server *or* There was no response	See Reason 4.
404 File or Object Not Found	See Reason 1 or 2. You've reached the server, but the URL doesn't refer to anything currently stored in it.
Broken Pipe *or* Document Contains No Data	Problem may be caused by a temporary communication breakdown between your browser and a server. Trying again often fixes the problem.

This activity introduces students to the basic terminology and features of a Web browser. It includes a reproducible activity worksheet for students. You may want to have your entire class complete the activity, even if many of your students already seem to be familiar with Web browser software. Doing so will ensure that everyone in the class uses the same terms to refer to the various parts of a browser.

Although students do not actually need to use a browser in order to complete the activity worksheet, the activity will be more clear to them if they fill out at least the second part of the worksheet while they are using a browser, or while they are watching one being demonstrated.

Objectives

- Students learn the terms commonly used to refer to the different parts of a Web browser.
- Students identify the functions of each of the parts of a Web browser.

Presentation

Hand out a copy of the activity worksheet to each student. Then, proceed with the activity based on the type of setting in which you choose to present it:

- *Computer lab with students seated alone or in pairs at computers:* Encourage students to use each of the browser's buttons, menu commands, and other parts as you walk them through the list of terms and functions on the worksheet. Move around the room to observe students as they complete the worksheet.
- *Regular classroom with a browser displayed (using a TV, monitor, or overhead projector):* Have students complete the worksheet as you name browser terms and demonstrate functions. Remember to stop and give students enough time to finish each part of the worksheet.
- *Regular classroom with no browser displayed:* Go over the first part of the worksheet in class. Ask students to finish the rest of the worksheet as homework, using computers elsewhere at your site or using home computers. Remind them to refer to the directions in the worksheet.

Directions

The suggestions below expand on the directions to students that appear in the worksheet.

Part One: Terms. You may want to use a question-and-answer format for this part of the activity. Encourage students to suggest terms for the different parts of the browser, but tell them to make sure that they write down only the terms listed in the second part of the worksheet.

Part Two: Functions. You may want to read aloud from the Web Research Essentials 2 handout on page 13 before students do this part of the worksheet. However, tell students that it is important for them to write descriptions of the functions of the browser in their own words—the words they would use if they needed to explain a browser to someone who had never used one. Students who run out of space on the front of the worksheet may write on the back.

Evaluation

Collect the worksheets, and use the Web Research Essentials 2 handout on page 13 to evaluate them. Note any responses that need to be corrected or clarified. Then, pass back the worksheets, and ask students to write corrections or clarifications to their own responses as you go over each part of the worksheet as a class. Students should keep their corrected worksheets in their notebooks for future reference.

NAME ______________________ CLASS ______________________ DATE ______________

ACTIVITY 2 Using a Browser Worksheet

Part One: Terms

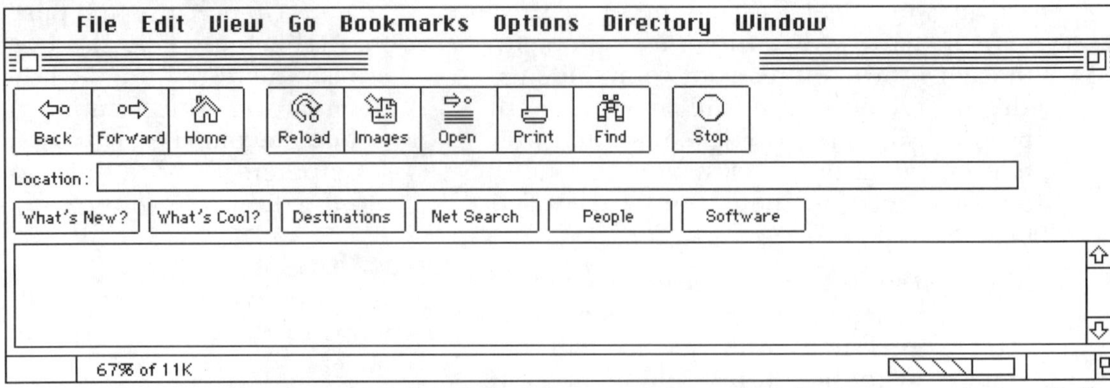

Using a colored pen or pencil, label each important part of the browser window below with one of the numbered terms from the list in Part Two.

Part Two: Functions

Write a description for the function of each of the parts of the browser listed below.

1. Toolbar Buttons

General description: ______________________

____

Individual buttons: ______________________

____

____

2. Menus

General description: ______________________

____

Individual menus and commands: ______________________

____

____

3. Directory Buttons: ______________________

4. Title Bar: ______________________

5. Location Window: ______________________

6. Main Window: ______________________

7. Status Line: ______________________

8. Progress Bar: ______________________

9. Scrollbar and Scroll Buttons: ______________________

PART THREE: SEARCH PARTY
Searching for Information on the World Wide Web

It's been said that the Web is like a card catalog into which anyone can walk up and drop a card. No one has the authority to screen everything that people "drop" on the Web, and no single organization maintains a complete catalog or index to everything that's available. Instead, people—everywhere, everyday—set up their own Web pages, and records for these pages show up in any of a number of competing Web indexes. Use this section of the *Teaching Notes* to introduce your students to the two most common types of indexes:

- Web search engines (pages 17–20)
- Web directories (page 21)

The information on search engines and directories is summarized for students in a handout. The same handout also offers suggestions on how to conduct successful searches:

Web Research Essentials 4: Directories and Search Engines at a Glance (page 22)

The section ends with materials for an activity to give students practice in using Web search tools to narrow a subject. (You can use the activity during an actual research project.) To conduct the activity, use the Teaching Guide on page 23, and this student worksheet:

Activity 3: Searching the Web (Worksheet, page 24)

Web Search Engines

A wide variety of Web sites allow students to use *search engines* to look for Web pages that contain keywords related to the subjects they're researching. When they use a search engine, students need to remember that they are not searching through every page on the Web each time they submit a query. Instead, they are accessing a very large computer-generated index at the search engine site they happen to be using. Each site compiles its index by periodically running a computer program, called a *robot, crawler,* or *spider,* that scours the Web looking for new pages to add to the site's index. Because the Web is constantly growing and changing, none of the sites can honestly claim to offer a complete index to its entire contents. Nonetheless, search engines are very powerful research tools.

Each of the search engine sites provides a basic search form on its home page. To activate the search engine, your students will type in keywords and click on a button, often labeled *Search.* The site then looks through its index for pages that contain the keywords. Figure 3-1 shows a portion of the form for the HotBot search engine (**www.hotbot.com**).

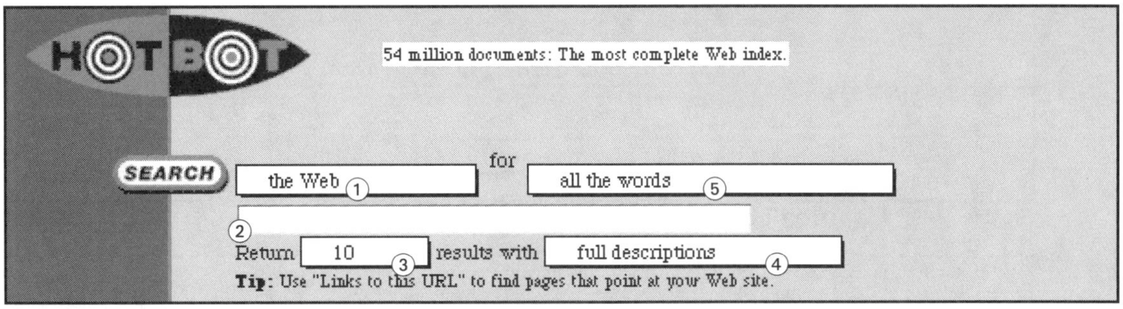

Figure 3-1: A portion of HotBot's search form

Some search engine forms provide pull-down menus to allow students to customize their searches. The first pull-down menu on HotBot's form (1) offers your students the option of conducting a search either of the Web or in an archive of Usenet newsgroup postings. (Beginners will want to keep the menu set to "the Web.") Just below the blank space on the keyword form (2) are two more pull-down menus. The one on the left (3) allows your students to specify whether they want to see just the first ten, twenty-five, fifty, seventy-five, or one hundred results of their search. The menu on the lower right (4) lets your students indicate whether they want to see full descriptions, brief descriptions, or just the addresses for the results that HotBot finds for their search. The final menu (5) is the one most often used. Figure 3-2 shows HotBot's search form with this menu pulled down.

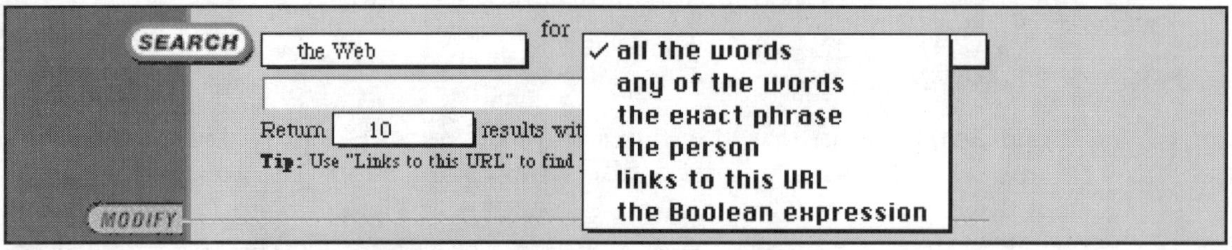

Figure 3-2: HotBot's search form with one menu pulled down

The first three menu options are the most helpful. Suppose that a student types in the keywords *foreign countries.* Selecting "any of the words" tells the search engine to look through its index for Web pages that contain either the word *foreign,* or the word *countries,* or both; selecting "all the words" tells the engine to find only pages that contain both *foreign* and *countries;* and selecting "the exact phrase" tells the engine to look for pages that contain the words as a group—*"foreign countries"*—in the same order in which they were typed in. Other HotBot menus allow your students to further customize searches, and a *Help* button (not shown) provides a link to tips on how to use the search engine.

Not all search engines have a basic search form that provides so many options. Some have a link to an "advanced" or "customized" search form, but most will require your students to include Boolean operators (AND, OR, NOT) and quotation marks or parentheses. (For more on Boolean operators and quotation marks, see the handout Web Research Essentials 4, on page 22.)

Using a Search Engine to Find Information

The search form for another popular search engine, Infoseek (**www.infoseek.com**), is shown in Figure 3-3.

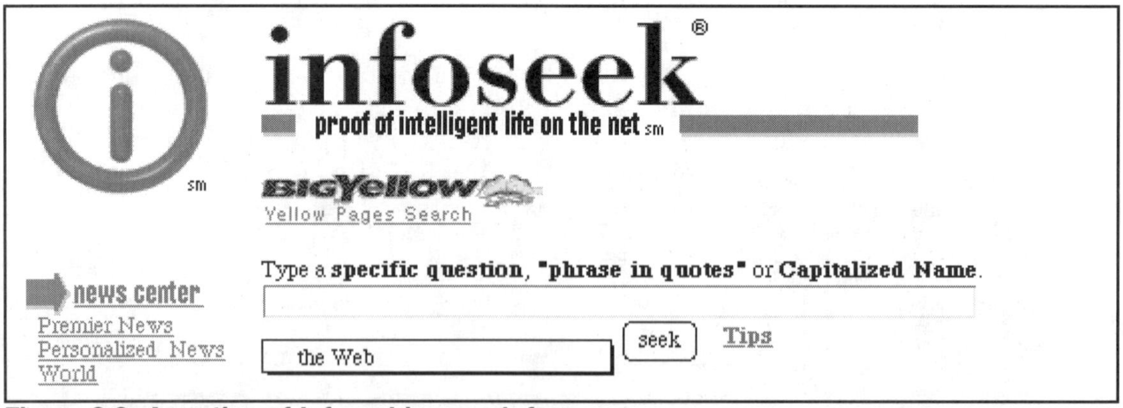

Figure 3-3: A portion of Infoseek's search form

It's not clear from the initial search form that appears on the screen whether the engine will look through its index for pages that contain all of the input keywords, pages that contain any one of them, or pages that contain the exact phrase typed in. One way to find out what the engine will look for is to try a search. Figure 3-4 shows the Infoseek search form with two keywords typed in.

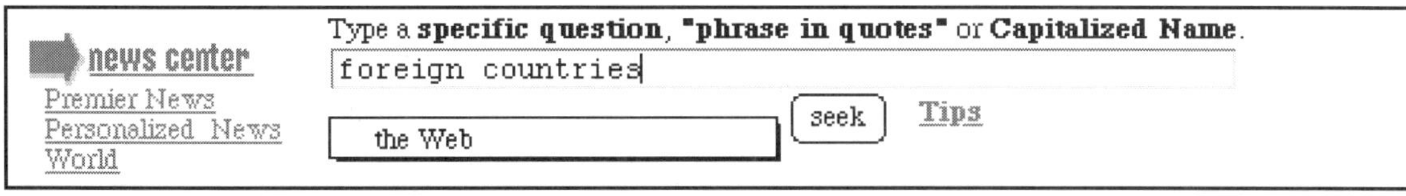

Figure 3-4: Search form with the keywords *foreign countries* typed in

A student who was looking for general background information on foreign countries might think it would make sense to type in *foreign countries* and click *seek*. Figure 3-5 shows the results from such a search.

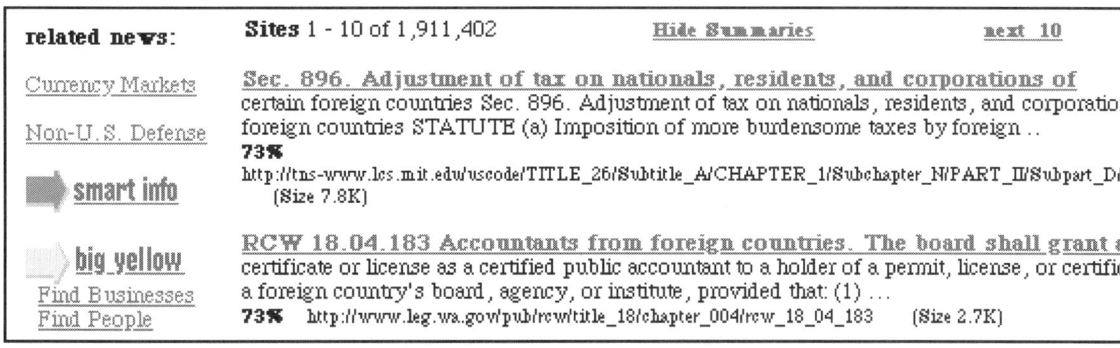

Figure 3-5: First two results of a search for the words *foreign countries*

Although Figure 3-5 doesn't show the whole results page as it would appear in a browser, it does show most of the important information the page contains. The total number of Web pages in Infoseek's index that match the query—almost two million—is shown at the top. Also shown are underlined hyperlinks to the two pages that Infoseek thinks are most likely to be the kind of page the student wanted to find. Each search engine uses a different set of criteria to decide how to rank its list of results for a search. As the abstract for the first result shows, Infoseek has given its highest relevancy ranking to a page on tax law. At first glance, this might seem a little bizarre. On closer inspection, though, it becomes clear that this page scored high for some very logical reasons: It contains both of the keywords in its title, and the keywords are repeated within the text of the page itself.

Unfortunately, unless the student who initiated this search happens to be studying accounting, tax law is probably not what he or she was looking for. Among the almost two million pages found by the search engine, there are probably a few pages that contain the kind of general information the student *did* want to find. However, figuring out where those pages might appear in the list of results would be an almost impossible task.

Refining a Search

The problem with this search is that it was not specific enough. Given only the words *foreign countries,* the search engine had no way of knowing that the student was looking for general background information. So, to cut down the number of results, the student might try adding the words *background information* to the search.

The student could narrow the search even further by checking the search engine's online help information. Next to the *seek* button on Infoseek's search form is a hyperlink labeled *Tips*. By clicking on it, and then clicking on the *Quick Reference* link on the next page that appears, students will discover that Infoseek requires them to put a plus sign (+) in front of all of the additional words that must appear in the Web pages they want to find. The illustration below shows all the keywords typed in, with plus signs added.

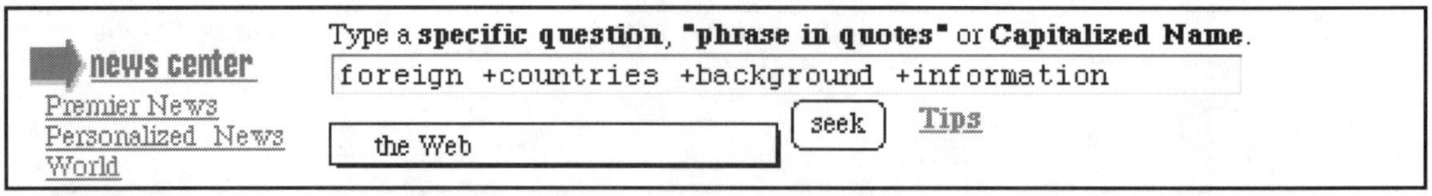

Figure 3-6: Search form with additional keywords and plus signs typed in

This tells the search engine to look only for pages that contain *all* of the keywords, in any order. The results of this search are shown in Figure 3-7.

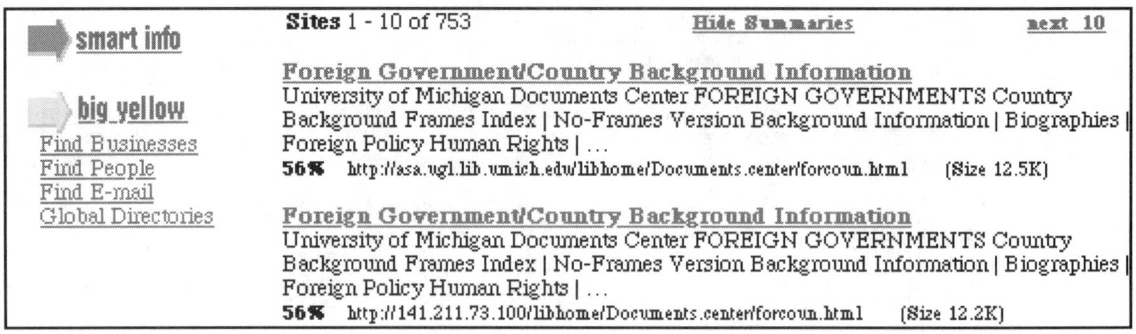

Figure 3-7: First two results of the revised search

The total number of Web pages matching the revised query is less than a thousand—down from almost two million—and a glance at the abstracts for the first two results shows that the student is much closer to locating the type of information he or she wanted to find.

Although the wording of this query produced good results with Infoseek, that doesn't mean it would work nearly as well with a different search engine. For one thing, each search engine uses a different set of criteria to rank its results. A different search engine that finds the same page ranked first by Infoseek may rank the page so low on *its* list of results that the student would never get to it. Also, search syntax (words and symbols used to narrow queries) is not always consistent across different search engines. However, the main differences are summarized in the handout Web Research Essentials 4 (page 22).

What Students Should Expect from Their Searches

A final note on search engines: You may want to remind students to be realistic about the quantity and quality of sources they hope to find from Web searches. Students shouldn't expect that a half an hour of searching on the Web will provide them with enough information to write a report. They may find that many of the pages they come across will be most useful as "steppingstones" to further study—similar to encyclopedia articles they might read in an early research stage but not refer to in their final reports. However, many Web pages, like encyclopedia articles, contain bibliographies or "Further Reading" lists that will lead students to books, articles, and other sources that explore their subjects in more depth. This doesn't mean that they won't be able to find *any* Web pages they can refer to directly as sources in a report—it just means that they shouldn't plan to write entire reports based only on information that they've found on the Web.

Web Directories

No matter how carefully students construct keyword searches, and no matter how thoughtfully they revise and narrow their searches, they will often end up with many more results than they have time to wade through. To anyone trying to find something quickly, the Web's greatest asset—the huge amount of information it contains—can also seem like its greatest liability. Remember the card catalog analogy? People are continuously adding pages to the Web, and search engine sites are mechanically indexing most of the pages. Even a carefully worded query can produce a list of results that contains many pages that aren't related at all to the subject the person who initiated the search had in mind.

Another Way to Search

Information overload became a problem on the Web soon after its inception. People responded by setting up browsable directories—catalogs of Web pages placed into a hierarchy of categories based on their subject matter. The current home page for one of the first of these sites, Yahoo (**www.yahoo.com**), is shown in Figure 3-8.

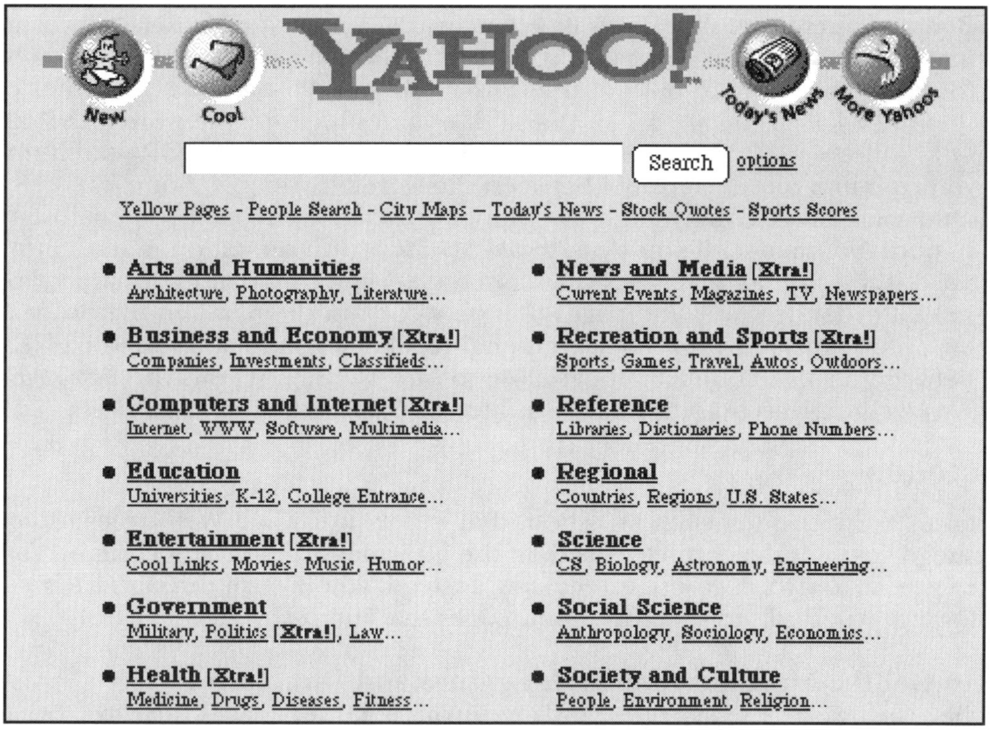

Figure 3-8: Home page for the Web directory Yahoo

Notice in Figure 3-8 that one of Yahoo's top-level categories is labeled *Regional*. Underneath it is a subcategory labeled *Countries*. A student who clicked on the *Countries* hyperlink would then see a page that includes links to information on more than two hundred countries. The student could browse through the list of countries, find the name of one that interested him or her, and click on its hyperlink to find Web pages that contain information about it—without ever typing in a single keyword. That's the feature that makes Web directories so useful—they're *browsable*.

Disadvantages

There are possible disadvantages to using a directory like Yahoo instead of a search engine site like HotBot. Because potential pages all have to be examined and categorized by human beings before they are placed into a directory—a time-and labor-intensive process—directories contain many fewer pages than the robot-generated indexes at search engine sites, and they're not quite as up-to-date.

WEB RESEARCH ESSENTIALS 4

Search Engines and Directories at a Glance

Search Engines

Search engines are tools that can be accessed at Web sites such as HotBot, Infoseek, AltaVista, Lycos, WebCrawler, or Excite. You type keywords into a form on the home page of one of these sites, and a search engine looks through the site's index of millions of Web pages to find only the pages that contain your keywords.

Search Forms

Most search forms are customizable. Here's why: Indexes at search sites are so large that simple searches can return too many results for anyone to look through. Therefore, search forms offer options for telling *how* you want a search engine to look for keywords. Some search forms require the use of **Boolean operators** and **quotation marks.**

- **Boolean operators.** When you type two words, *foreign* and *countries,* for example, into a search engine, you may also indicate whether you want the engine to look for pages that contain both of the words (*foreign AND countries*), or either of them (*foreign OR countries*). Most search engines look for the words AND and OR, but some (like Infoseek) assume that you want to do an OR search unless you type in a plus (+) symbol between the words (foreign +countries).
- **Quotation marks.** Many engines will look for exact phrases if you enclose them in quotation marks. If you type *"Pablo Neruda"* (with quotation marks) into Infoseek, it will find all the pages that contain Neruda's first and last names, together in that order. It won't find pages that only contain the name in the order *Neruda, Pablo.* AltaVista, another search engine, allows you to add the word NEAR between terms that must appear close to one another. If you type *Pablo NEAR Neruda* into AltaVista, it will also find pages that contain *Neruda, Pablo.*

Directories

Directories are Web sites, such as Yahoo, that index individual Web pages using multilevel categories or "subject trees" based on the information the pages contain. You don't need to type in keywords to use directories. Instead, you browse through their contents by following hyperlinks to categories and pages that interest you.

How to Get the Most out of Search Engines and Directories

- Begin a research session by browsing through a directory. If the directory lists a page that contains the kind of information you need, you'll have saved yourself a lot of time. If it doesn't, you can always move on to a search engine.
- Always look through the online help information for any directory or search engine you plan to use. Before you begin a search, become familiar with the search options the site offers and the search syntax it requires.
- When using a search engine, start by trying a focused search with very specific keywords. If you find that the search produces too few results, or none at all, try broadening the search a little by including synonyms for the original keywords or by using keywords that are more general.
- Each directory has a different structure for categorizing pages, and each search engine has its own criteria for ranking results. If you can't find what you need using one search engine or directory, try another. You may get much better results.
- Remember that you don't need to have made a final decision about your subject before you begin a search. The Web can help you brainstorm. Directories, in particular, can be especially helpful in guiding you toward a topic.

ACTIVITY 3 Searching the Web Teaching Guide

This activity gives students practice in using common Web search tools. You can use it in the context of an actual research project, to help students narrow their subjects and to find preliminary information on them. Students will need to have access to Internet-connected, browser-equipped computers in order to complete the accompanying worksheet.

Objectives

- Students conduct a keyword search using a Web search engine.
- Students use a Web directory to find information on a specific subject.
- Students locate online help information and use it to refine a keyword search.
- Students narrow their subjects using the results of their searches.

Presentation

After handing out a copy of the activity worksheet to each student, walk students through the step-by-step directions below. Students can then refer to the directions on the worksheet to complete it independently, using computers elsewhere at your site, or using home computers. However, you may want to present this activity in a computer lab setting, so that you can monitor the progress of your students as they search, and help when needed.

Directions

The suggestions below expand on the directions to students that appear in the worksheet.

Part One: Using a Search Engine

1. Students may need synonyms in case the search engine doesn't return good results for their original keywords.
2. A list of search engines appears at the end of Appendix B (page 47).
3. Remind students to check the spelling of their keywords. Students are likely to choose keywords that produce too many results. Tell them this is OK at this point, because they will be able to refine their searches in the next step.
4. Depending on which search engine they choose, students may need to add Boolean operators (page 22), symbols, or quotation marks.
5. Students should write down the number for their first refined search, not any subsequent ones.
6. Remind students that using a search engine is a trial-and-error process; they may need to refine their searches several times before they get satisfactory results.

Part Two: Using a Web Directory

1. A list of Web directories appears at the end of Appendix B (page 47).
2. Inform students that they may need to look through several top-level categories before they find one that contains what they are looking for.
3. Tell students that at this point they are only looking for a subcategory inside the directory, not a Web page outside it. Inform them that if the first part (hostname) of the URL for this step doesn't match the first part of the URL in step two, they have reached an outside page and need to click the Back button until the first parts of the URLs match again. Students who can't find information on their research subjects should browse through the directory until they reach an alternate subcategory that interests them, and list its URL instead.
4. Remind students that the first part of a URL for an outside page will differ from the first part of the URL for the directory.

Part Three: Using Search Results

1. Students should look through the pages for a few minutes before writing their descriptions. Those who found pages that didn't give them any ideas for narrowing their subjects should instead describe what they learned while searching.

Evaluation

See the Answer Keys on page 52.

NAME ______________________ CLASS ________________ DATE __________

ACTIVITY 3 Searching the Web Worksheet

Part One: Using a Web Search Engine

1. Choose a subject about which you would like to find information: ____________

2. List keywords and synonyms or other words related to your subject: ____________

____

3. Choose a search engine to use to look for pages that contain your keywords. List its name and URL: ____

____

4. Use a browser to get to the search engine you have chosen. Type your keywords into the search engine form. List the number of results it returns: ______________

5. On the search engine site's home page, find a hyperlink to online help information. Read through it to learn how you can refine your search. Describe the adjustments you will make to get fewer results (if you found too many) or more results (if you found too few): ____

____

____

6. Type in your refined search and list the number of results it returns: __________

7. Continue refining your search until you find a page containing information you can use. (If needed, use the synonyms and words you listed in step one.) List the page's title and URL: ____

Part Two: Using a Web Directory

1. Choose a directory in which to look for information on your subject from Part One. List its URL: ____

2. Use a browser to get to the directory you have chosen. Look at the list of top-level categories on the site's home page, and choose at least one in which to look for information on your subject. List the category or categories: ______________

3. Click on a top-level category, and follow hyperlinks until you find a subcategory that includes your subject. (Remember to look for synonyms or related words also.) List the subcategory's URL: ____

4. Look through the subcategory to find an outside Web page related to your subject. List the page's title and URL: ____

____

Part Three: Using Search Results

1. Describe an aspect of your subject, discussed somewhere in the pages you've found, that might lead to a good, focused topic for a research report: ______________

____

PART FOUR: WHO SAYS SO, ANYWAY?
Evaluating Sources on the World Wide Web

This section contains information on the following topics related to the evaluation of Web sites during research:

- criteria for evaluating Web sites as information sources (pages 25–30)
- information on analyzing URLs (page 29)
- guidelines for classifying different types of Web sites (page 31)

The standard criteria for evaluating Web sites and the guidelines for identifying different types of Web sites are reproduced on two student handouts:

- Web Research Essentials 5: Source Evaluation Criteria (page 30)
- Web Research Essentials 6: Types of Web Sites (page 31)

At the end of the section is an activity that your students can use to evaluate potential information sources they have located on the Web. To conduct this activity, use the following materials:

Activity 4: Evaluating Web Sources, Teaching Guide and Worksheet (pages 32–33)

Why Web Sites Need to Be Evaluated

Earlier in this book, we mentioned that the World Wide Web is like a giant card catalog into which anyone can drop a card. For the same reasons that this wide-open system can make finding information on the Web challenging, evaluating the information that you do find can also be a challenge. After all, anyone can publish a Web page, for any reason—to inform, to disinform, to preach, to sell something, to express opinions, to shape public opinion, or to share pictures of pets. Given that there is no gatekeeping system that keeps "bad" sites out while letting "good" sites in, evaluating Web sites might seem like a monumental task, demanding that the Web user develop a whole new set of standards, or criteria.

Luckily, the criteria needed to evaluate Web sites are not very different from the criteria that should be used to evaluate any information source, print or nonprint. These traditional criteria involve examining the author's credentials, the objectivity and accuracy of the information, and the uniqueness and date of the source. The chart on page 30 outlines these five standard criteria in the form of questions you and your students should ask about the source, and it points out some special considerations involved in applying these criteria to Web sites. Guidelines for applying the five standard criteria to Web sites are discussed in more detail on the following pages.

How Web Sites Are Used

How your students plan to use the information in a Web site influences how strictly they need to evaluate it. Below are some reasons for using a site.

- to get ideas for a research topic
- to find information about books or other resources related to the research topic
- to find links to other Web sites related to the research topic
- to get opinions about a controversy related to the research topic
- to get information that can be verified through other sources
- to quote a group's or individual's opinion on an issue
- to get authoritative or definitive information

To use the Web site for the last of the reasons given—that is, to cite the Web site as a source in itself—your students should be able to find satisfactory answers to all of the following questions. On a cautionary note, you may be surprised to find how few sites actually do meet all the criteria. However, this failure to meet the standards of printed material is not surprising when the newness of the World Wide Web is taken into account. Universal standards for any medium take time to evolve, and the standards for Web sites are still in the evolutionary phase. In the meantime, you and your students may find that the many sites are most useful as pointers to other, more authoritative sources of information.

Standard Criteria for Evaluating Information Sources[1]

Coverage: What topics are covered in the site, in how much depth are they covered, and how unique is the coverage?

The question of *coverage* is the first one your students should address. To determine whether a site offers adequate coverage, students should ask themselves these questions:

- Does the Web site offer the kind of coverage I am looking for?
- Would I be better off getting this information from the tried-and-true reference books in the library, or does the site contain a type and depth of coverage not available elsewhere?
- Does the site contain enough of the type of information I am looking for? (Many sites on the Web, for example, are "under construction" and don't contain complete information.)

Considering the time your students will need to spend verifying the reliability of a source—not to mention the cost in time and money of being online—Web sites should be pursued as sources only if they appear to provide unique coverage.

In the videotape, we evaluated four sites, each dealing with the topic of Romani culture. How do these sites measure up to the coverage criterion? All of the pages are complete sources, and all do a fairly good job of covering the topics they set out to cover. Also, along with reading lists they provide, the *Romani Rights* and *The Patrin* sites both contain many outside hyperlinks to related sites that could prove to be useful. Since the *Britannica* site is an online version of the printed encyclopedia series, you might prefer to have your students use the current printed version if they have access to it. However, features such as the online search function make the *Britannica* site an attractive alternative to the print source.

Accuracy: Is the information in the Web site accurate?

Accuracy is another major criterion for evaluating information sources. The old adage that you can't believe everything you read is more relevant than ever in the age of the Internet, where anyone can be a publisher. Caution your students not to assume that information on the Web is accurate; they must attempt to check a site's accuracy. Determining accuracy can be difficult. In some cases, it's easy to tell that a source is not accurate: For example, a source that contains many typographical or grammatical errors should be avoided. However, the fact that a site is beautifully constructed and is free from obvious errors is no guarantee of its accuracy. There are a number of strategies your students can use to evaluate the accuracy of information found at a site:

- Examine the authorship of the page; if the author is an expert on the topic, the source is more likely to be accurate. (See the next page for more on authority.)

---

[1] The criteria listed in this section, and the discussion that follows them, have been adapted from information in the Web site *Teaching Critical Evaluation Skills for World Wide Web Resources*, created by Jan Alexander and Marsha Tate of the Wolfgram Memorial Library, Widener University. This site can be accessed by selecting the link "Evaluating Web Resources" from the page at http://www.widener.edu/libraries.html/).

- Check for acknowledgments[2] that cite reliable sources or that indicate that the information in the Web site has undergone an editorial review process.
- Compare the information in the site to other, reliable information sources.
- Examine claims made in the source to see that they are backed up with reasoned arguments and verifiable evidence. Sites full of unsupported claims and undocumented facts should be avoided.

Most of the pages shown in the evaluation section of the video don't cite sources for the specific pieces of factual information they contain. However, both the *Britannica Online* site and the Library of Congress site have links to information that describe the review process used to verify their contents. The Library of Congress page, for example, includes Acknowledgments indicating the names of researchers and other reviewers, so it's clear that the site has undergone some editorial scrutiny before being published. Furthermore, the content of all four sites is fairly well written and is free from grammar, usage, and mechanics errors. Yet there are some discrepancies in facts between the pages. For example, the Britannica page estimates that there are two to three million Romani in the world, the Library of Congress page estimates three to six million, and the Patrin page estimates ten million. Because the data on the Romani population varies so widely in these three sources, students should look in at least one other reliable source to verify which figure is most accurate.

Authority: Who is the author, and what are his or her qualifications? What is the reputation of the publisher?

If your students plan to cite the Web in a research report, they should be able to rely on the authority of the site. That is, they ought to be able to determine the credentials of the person or group who created and published it. Evidence that a site's author is qualified to write on a certain topic might include the following:

- a graduate degree in the field he or she is writing about
- a list of other publications written by the author on the same topic, including print publications
- a job title indicating that the author is involved in the field he or she is writing about—as an employee of a reputable firm, institution, or government agency, for example.

Finding information on the author can be difficult. If your students have found a Web page through a search engine, they might not have arrived at the site's home page, where links to information about the author and publisher are most likely to be found. However, a well-constructed Web page should show the user how to get back to the home page. From there, the user may have to follow several hyperlinks to find the author or authors' qualifications, but a well-documented site should make its author(s) fairly easy to discover. Even if no information is given about the author, most Web sites will include an address to which you or your students can direct inquiries.

Even if detailed information about the author is not provided, the reputation of the publisher may be enough to validate a promising Web site. Encyclopaedia Britannica and the Library of Congress, for example, publish two of the sites mentioned in the *Research on the Internet* video; both of these institutions are well known as reliable information providers, so information from their Web sites may be regarded as being as reliable as information from their printed publications. Both *The Patrin* site and the *Romani Rights* site lack adequate information about their authors. Also, both appear to be self-published; there is no identifiable publisher or sponsor backing these pages. Unless it's possible to verify the information on these two sources in other reliable sources, a researcher would have to be very careful about citing factual information

---

[2] If the publisher has included acknowledgments, they are usually fairly easy to find. Sometimes the home page provides a link labeled "Acknowledgments" or "Credits." In other cases, the credits, or a link to them, may be given at the end of particular informative pages within the site.

directly from them. Both pages, however, contain valuable links to other sites and printed materials—many more than either the Library of Congress site or the *Britannica Online* site provide.

Currency: How current is the information in the site?

A surprising number of sites do not indicate when the information they contain was created, when it was published, and when it was last revised. For example, none of the Romani-related sites in the videotape provide complete information on the date of creation, publication, or revision. Although, in light of their publishers, the *Britannica Online* and Library of Congress pages can be considered fairly up-to-date, it is difficult to tell when the information on the sites was first created and when the sites were last revised. The Britannica page contains a 1996 copyright, so a researcher can probably assume that the page mirrors information in the 1996 print edition of the encyclopedia. The Patrin home page contains a "last updated" line, but no information on when the information was first created. The *Romani Rights* page has a creation date, but no "last updated" line. The *Romani Rights* and *The Patrin* sites, however, both provide fairly current annotated lists of print sources to consult for more information.

It is good Web publishing practice to provide full publication date information. In reality, most Web sites don't provide you with all of this information. However, your students may not need to eliminate a site based on incomplete publication data, especially if the site measures up against the other criteria. The currency of the information is important, however, if the research subject is time-sensitive. For example, a site that gives crime statistics for a certain city but doesn't provide a date for those statistics—or provides statistics that are out of date—will not be very useful. When posting and revision dates are provided, they usually appear near the bottom of the home page.

Objectivity: How objective is the information?

The *objectivity* of the information in a Web site can never be taken for granted. People and groups have various *agendas,* or underlying purposes, for publishing on the Web. One reason people and organizations publish Web sites is to provide information; other reasons might be to sell things or to promote a cause. Many sites mix information with advertisements or calls to action. Sites like these don't necessarily need to be ruled out; the information they contain may be accurate and authoritative. However, students must be aware of the Web site's purpose. If the purpose of the site is to persuade people to think a certain way about an issue, then students should ask themselves what the other side of that issue is. They should then look for information on that other side.

Also, in reviewing any site, students must realize that every publication has some degree of bias. That is, the information and the way it is presented usually reflect the values of its author or of its sponsor (that is, the person or group, other than the author, whose money has gone into the creation and maintenance of the site). If a site has a sponsor other than the author, it should provide a way to contact the sponsor.

Of the four sites mentioned in the video, two appear to have sponsors: *Britannica Online* and the Library of Congress site. The first sponsor is a publishing company, the second is the U.S. government. Because the *Britannica Online* site is sponsored by a company whose stated mission is to provide information on a broad range of topics, it is likely that it provides fairly unbiased information. Because the Library of Congress is sponsored by a democratically elected government representing all U.S. citizens, it too can be considered a relatively unbiased source.

The other two pages, *Romani Rights* and *The Patrin,* appear to be self-published; that is, they have no sponsor. However, the bias of their authors must still be evaluated. The author of the *Romani Rights* site indicates that her site is intended as a clearinghouse for information from Romani organizations, particularly those concerned about Romani human and civil rights. Similarly, the author of *The Patrin* includes in his site a sort of mission statement that reveals the page's purpose, which is to heighten public awareness of Romani culture and the Romani struggle for rights. Sites like *The Patrin* and *Romani*

Rights, which advocate a cause, tend to be somewhat one-sided. However, because these two sites make no attempt to hide their biases, students can still evaluate the pages effectively. If the sites appear to be accurate, authoritative, and current enough, students may use them as sources for information. However, students conducting research would need to use other, more objective sources as well.

To evaluate the degree and type of bias in a Web site, it helps to know something about Web sites' URLs, or Uniform Resource Locators.

What's in a Name? The Uniform Resource Locator. Earlier in this booklet, we discussed the different parts of the Uniform Resource Locator (URL). The URL is a handy code that lets computers exchange information. But you don't need to be a computer to read a URL; in fact, you and your students can learn quite a bit about a Web site before you even open it, just by examining its URL. For purposes of evaluation, you should pay particular attention to the hostname and pathname of a URL. You'll remember that the hostname (the last part of the section that follows the protocol code) contains one of the following codes: *com, edu, gov, mil, net,* or *org.* For information on what each of these codes means, see Web Research Essentials 1 (page 10).

Following the first slash after the hostname, the URL may include a path. Frequently, you can tell whether the page is a personal page by examining the path. For example, in *edu* sites, paths often begin with a tilde (~), followed by a name or initials identifying the person responsible for that site. For personal home pages on commercial or network service providers (*com* or *net*), paths often begin with something like "People" or "Users." The part of that path may indicate the name of the Web site's creator.

Types of Web Sites. As your students begin to evaluate the objectivity of a Web site, it will be helpful to have them classify the site into one of these five categories: *advocacy, sales/marketing, informational, news,* or *personal.* The site's URL may provide enough information to categorize a site; in most cases, however, students will need to look at the body of the site to be sure of its type. Web Research Essentials 6 (page 31) describes each type of site and also provides guidelines for determining the level of objectivity in each type.

Other Criteria

Of course, in any medium, specific evaluation criteria exist. The medium of the World Wide Web offers its own special problems and its own shortcut evaluation methods.

User-Friendliness

Evaluating a site based on its user-friendliness is largely a matter of personal preference. If you can't navigate the site, for example, or if you've been annoyed by how long it has taken to load images that turn out to be pointless, chances are you will simply move on to another site. However, if you plan to recommend a site for your students to view, you may want to evaluate its user-friendliness more carefully. For example, pay attention to how the Web site uses graphics. Since graphics can load slowly, many Web users prefer to leave the graphics-loading function of their browsers off while they surf, turning graphics on only when they find a graphic they want to view. It's helpful if the graphics on a Web site are well labeled so that the viewer can decide whether or not to download them. Also, Web sites that depend entirely on image maps for navigation will be difficult to use if the image-loading option is turned off.

Stability

One of the advantages of the World Wide Web is its immediacy; current information on all topics is being added all the time. The flip side of the Web's currency is its temporality; many sites don't last long. A Web site's stability is a concern, but it is not something the researcher has much control over. The best Web sites change because a "Webmaster" updates and improves them. Many Web sites simply disappear. The best way for a student to guard against the instability of a Web source he or she has cited is to make a hard copy or a disk copy of the Web page. For more information on copying Web pages, see Web Research Essentials 2 (page 13).

WEB RESEARCH ESSENTIALS 5
Source Evaluation Criteria

CRITERIA	RELATED QUESTIONS	CONSIDERATIONS FOR THE WEB SITE
1 **Coverage** refers to the extent of coverage of topics and to the availability of the same information in other sources.	How unique is the coverage of information in the source?	Many Web sites contain information that can be found just as easily in library reference books.
2 **Accuracy** refers to the reliability of the information in the source (based, for example, on the use of editors) and to the verifiability of the information (that is, through the inclusion of documentation or other source credits).	Does the source cite references for the factual information it provides? Can the information in the source be verified in other sources? Does the source contain obvious inaccuracies? Is the author or publisher of the information reliable? (See *Authority*, below.)	The accuracy of information in many Web sites is difficult to establish. Sites that contain blatant inaccuracies should be rejected. Sites to be used as primary information sources should include acknowledgment of information sources, expert authorship, and/or evidence of an editorial review process.
3 **Authority** refers to the qualifications of the author and the reputation of the publisher.	Does the author appear to be qualified to write on this topic? Does the publisher have a good reputation?	Authority can be very difficult to establish. Virtually anyone can publish his or her own Web page. Even if the author's name is listed, his or her qualifications often are not. In most cases, an e-mail address (which does not necessarily reveal the author's real name) is provided.
4 **Currency** refers to the presence or absence of complete information on the original publication date, and to the date of revisions, if any.	How up-to-date is the information in the source?	Information on the date of creation and the date of the last revision of a Web site may be found near the bottom of the home page. Many sites do not provide this information.
5 **Objectivity** refers to the extent of bias in the publication, as well as the presence or absence of a persuasive aim.	How objective is the information in the source? What is the bias of the author or publisher? Is the author trying to persuade you to think a certain way or to buy a certain product?	A Web site can generally be placed into one of the following categories: *advocacy, sales/marketing, informational, news, personal.* Identifying the type of page is the first step toward evaluating objectivity. (See page 31.)

This table is based on a method for evaluating Web resources developed by Jan Alexander and Marsha Tate (http://www.widener.edu/libraries.html/).

WEB RESEARCH ESSENTIALS 6
Types of Web Sites

Advocacy Web pages often include the domain type *org* (or *com* followed by an individual's or group's name). The purpose of advocacy pages is to shape or sway public opinion, often about controversial issues.

Advocacy pages can be informative, but their objectivity needs to be evaluated. To be considered a source, *an advocacy site must clearly state its goals and the name of its sponsoring organization.* If an advocacy page does these things and meets the general criteria on page 30, it can be used as a source. However, you must be sure to (1) distinguish **fact** from **opinion** in the information you take from such pages, and (2) state in your research paper that the information came from an advocacy group's page. **In many cases, you will find that advocacy pages are best used as links to other, more suitable sources.**

Business/marketing Web pages These pages' URLs usually include the name of the business plus the domain type *com.* These are commercial Web sites whose primary purpose is to advertise or sell goods or services.

A commercial site may be a useful source of information about its own products or services if it meets the general criteria on page 30 and if

- the identity of the company sponsoring the site is clear
- the informative sections of the site are clearly separated from the advertising sections

In addition, look on a company's home page for links to outside sources, such as consumer groups, that can validate the company's claims about its products.

Informational Web pages frequently include the domain type *gov* or *edu* in their URLs; that is, they often come from the servers of government or educational institutions. The purpose of an informational page is to provide information. Reports, schedules, directories, and encyclopedias are examples of informational sites that can be found on the Web.

Informational Web pages can be used as sources if they meet the criteria on page 30, the page's sponsor is identified, and the relationship of the sponsor to the site is known.

CAUTION: The fact that a site appears on a government or educational institution's server does not mean that that the information on the page is reliable. Anyone—a professor, a student, or a staff member—can publish a site on a college's or university's server. You must look for authority, accuracy, currency, and coverage with these sites just as with any other site.

News Web pages have URLs that include the name of the news outlet in the domain, followed by *com* or *org.* News pages, like *The Washington Post*'s site, provide current information.

News sites can be used as information sources if they meet the general criteria outlined on page 30 and if

- the identity of the company or organization sponsoring the page is clear
- advertisements in the site are clearly distinguished from news

Since journalists who write news stories often are not experts on their topics, news outlets are generally not as valuable to a researcher as more substantial information sources. News sources are most useful when you need extremely up-to-date information on a topic.

Personal home pages have URLs that can include any of the suffixes above, often followed by a slash, a tilde (~), and a personal name.

In general, unless a personal page fits into the category of an advocacy page or an informational page, it should not be used as an information source. However, many personal home pages, especially those that function as advocacy pages or informational pages, may provide pointers to other good sources of information.

This table is based on a method for evaluating Web resources developed by Jan Alexander and Marsha Tate (http://www.widener.edu/libraries.html/).

ACTIVITY 4 — Evaluating Web Sources Teaching Guide

This lesson focuses on evaluating sources that students have found in their research on the World Wide Web. The activity can be handled as a mini-lesson and incorporated into a unit on writing a research report; the worksheet on the following page can be used as a checklist for evaluating all electronic sources.

Objectives

- Students categorize their ideas about "what makes a good Web site" into the traditional criteria.
- Students evaluate their Web sites according to the standard criteria.

Presentation

Have each student or cooperative group identify a Web site that might be a promising information source. Pass out the Site Evaluation Form, one for each student or group. Instruct students to fill out the top part of the form, then to stop when they get to question 1.

Warm students up to the activity by asking them what makes them think the sites they have identified are "good" sites. Write their responses on the board or on an overhead transparency. Students may offer insights like these:

- The site is written or published by a well-known author or publisher.
- The site is packed with information.
- The site is current because it is on the Web.
- The site is well written, with no spelling or grammar mistakes.
- The site doesn't have ads.

Next, write the following six terms on the board, in the form of chart headings: *accuracy, authority, coverage, currency, objectivity.* Explain that the terms are criteria, or standards, for evaluating information sources on the Web. The meaning of each term appears on the chart on page 30. During this discussion, you may want to refer to the chart and to share the chart with your class. NOTE: The chart does not deal with the technical features, like graphics or user-friendliness, that are more personal, subjective criteria than the others.

Next, help students classify their earlier comments with respect to the six terms on the board; help them refine their comments about each criterion if necessary. If students have expressed weak criteria for what makes a good, reliable Web site, try to steer them to stronger criteria. (The statement that the Web site was up-to-date because it was on the Web is an example of a weak criterion.)

Activity

After discussing all the criteria, have students begin evaluating their sources. In many cases, they will not be able to answer the questions quickly but will need to read the body of the Web site carefully. The criteria are addressed in the questions as follows:

Coverage: 1, 2
Currency: 3
Authority: 4–6
Accuracy: 7, 8
Objectivity: 9, 10

If students have trouble understanding any of these questions, the information on the chart should be helpful.

All students should answer question 14 based on how trustworthy their site seems after they complete the form.

Challenge Activity

Questions 11–13 are advanced questions that deal with the issues of objectivity and bias in information sources. Although most students should recognize that a page published by a retail business may be trying to sell something, an advocacy page published by a nonprofit organization may be more difficult for younger students to evaluate. They may not have heard of the organization, and they may assume that its purpose is to inform. Younger students should probably be allowed to deal with the issue of objectivity by thinking carefully about questions 4, 9, and 10.

Evaluation

Guidelines for responding to the worksheet appear on page 52.

NAME ____________ CLASS ____________ DATE ____________

ACTIVITY 4 Evaluating Web Sources

Worksheet

Site Name: ____________ URL: ____________

Date Web site was first posted: ____________

Date Web site was last revised: ____________

Essential Evaluation Questions

1. Why are you interested in using this site? What will it add to your research?

____

2. Can you find the same information in a library book? ____________

3. Explain whether you think the information on the site is recent enough.

____

4. Who is the author or publisher of the Web site? (An author's name must be the full name, not a nickname or code name.) ____________

____

5. What is the address of the author or publisher? (You must be able to find a real address or an e-mail address.) ____________

____

6. Why do you think this author or publisher is or is not qualified to write on this topic? ____________

____

7. Does the site contain errors in spelling or grammar, or any other inaccuracies that you know of? ____________

8. Are you confident that the information in the source is reliable? ____________

Why or why not? ____________

____

9. What is the purpose of the page? Is it to provide news or information? to publicize someone's cause? to sell a product? Or is it a personal home page with links to various subjects that interest the page's author? Describe the purpose of the page. (The page may have a combination of purposes.)

____

____

10. Does the author seem to have a bias? If so, explain what you think it is.

____

____

Advanced Evaluation Questions

11. Do you know who sponsors (pays for the creation and upkeep of) the page? (The page's sponsor is not always the author; sometimes the sponsor is a company or nonprofit organization.) ____________

____

12. If the sponsor is a company or another type of organization, what is its primary business or purpose? ____________

____

13. Can you think of any reason that the sponsor's business might bias the information in the site? ____________

Your Conclusions

14. Do you think you should use this site as a primary source of information? Why or why not? ____________

____

If not, can the site be useful in any other way? How? ____________

____

APPENDIX A: DOCUMENTING INTERNET SOURCES

Whenever your students use information from an online source in their research papers, they must document that source both in the text and in their Works Cited lists, just as they would document any other information source. The following guide provides two alternate citation formats. One is based on the style of the Modern Language Association (MLA). The other is based on the style of the American Psychological Association (APA). Pages 34 to 39 contain detailed guidelines for using both styles. You may want to give copies of these pages to your students—or, to provide students with a more condensed version of the guidelines, you may prefer to distribute the following handouts:

- Web Research Essentials 7: A Quick Reference to MLA Documentation Style for Internet Sources (page 40)
- Web Research Essentials 8: A Quick Reference to APA Documentation Style for Internet Sources (page 41)

Appendix A also provides the following worksheet, which students can use to keep track of documentation information as they gather Internet sources for their research.

Activity 5: Web Source Log (page 42)

Where Is the Information That Should Be Included in Citations?

Publication information for an online source may appear at the beginning or end of the document or in a file attached to the document. **Note:** To keep track of the documentation, students should, if possible, save copies of all electronic documents they plan to cite. This information can be printed out or saved to a disk, preferably both. The advantage of a hard-copy printout is that the Internet address (URL) can be set to print automatically. (Each browser is different, but each should have a page-setup option that tells the printer to include various types of information in the header or footer, including the URL.) An Internet source that is saved to a disk will not automatically include that source's URL. If your students don't have access to printers, or if you want to be sure that they have a backup for the documentation from which they will need to cite sources, you can have students log the documentation for relevant Internet sources on the form on page 42.

What If Full Documentation Information Is Not Available?

A source may not provide all the publication information that a citation format calls for. For example, online reference sources, such as Britannica Online, usually do not give an author's name, and many Internet sources do not give full print publication information. Also, some of the information that a citation format calls for may not apply to particular sources. In such cases, students should include in their citations whatever relevant information is available.

Citing Sources in Text

When students quote or paraphrase information from another source in the text of their research reports, they must acknowledge the source of the information. The author of the source should be acknowledged, either directly in the text or in a parenthetical citation, along with the page number (MLA) or year of publication (APA), so that a reader can find the full citation for the source on the Works Cited page. Many Internet sources do not identify an author. In such a case, use a shortened version of the document title or the name of the Web page. Following are examples of parenthetical citations. The first is for a reference to a Web page in the *Sí, Spain* Web site. The second is for a Web page called "A Brief History of the Roma" within a Web site called *The Patrin.*

MLA: However, for the Romani in Spain, "the traditional pattern of segregation is increasingly difficult to maintain in urban areas . . ." (Barrio). [Since this site provides no page numbers, only the author's name is given in parentheses.]

According to the author of Romani advocacy Web site *The Patrin,* many Romani do not claim their ethnic heritage ("Brief History"). [When a title, rather than an author, is used within a parenthetical citation, the name of the article may be shortened. Again, since the site has no page numbers, none are provided here.]

APA: However, for the Romani in Spain, "the traditional pattern of segregation is increasingly difficult to maintain in urban areas . . ." (Barrio). [Since this site provides no publication date, only the author's name is given in parentheses.]

According to the author of Romani advocacy Web site *The Patrin,* many Romani do not claim their ethnic heritage ("Brief History," 1997).

MLA Style for Documenting Internet Sources in the Works Cited List

The MLA style for documenting sources in the Works Cited list makes a major distinction between sources that have a print version and sources that do not. Examples based on MLA style for various sources are provided below and on the following pages. In all cases the electronic address (URL) is optional, but we highly recommend its inclusion.

Internet Sources That Have Print Versions

Author's Last Name, First Name. "Title of Document, Article, or Part of a Work." <u>Title of Print Source</u>. Print Publication Information. Publication Medium [use the word *Online*]. <u>Database Title.</u> [or] Name of Electronic Library or Archive. Name of Computer Network. Date Information Was Accessed. electronic address, preceded by the word *Available.*

▼ ***Note:*** If an electronic address breaks onto a second line, divide the address immediately before one of the punctuation marks within it. Do not use a hyphen or any other mark of punctuation to divide the address.

Online Book or Play That Has a Print Version

After a book's title, which is followed by a period, include the following print publication information: Volume number (if any). City of Print Publication: Publisher, year of publication.

Christie, Agatha. <u>The Mysterious Affair at Styles.</u> London: Bodley Head, 1920. Online. Bartleby Library. Internet. 6 March 1997. Available http://www.columbia.edu/acis/bartleby/christie/.

Online Reference Work That Has a Print Version

After a reference work's title, which is followed by a period, include the following print publication information: edition. year of publication.

"Romany Language." <u>Encyclopædia Britannica.</u> 15th ed. 1974-1996. Online. <u>Britannica Online</u>. World Wide Web. 20 February 1997. Available http://www.eb.com:180/.

Online Article from a Magazine That Has a Print Version

After a magazine's title, include the following print publication information: Date: pages.

Kluger, Jeffrey. "Volcanoes with an Attitude." Time 24 Feb. 1997: n. pag. Online. World Wide Web. 20 Feb. 1997. Available http://pathfinder.com/time/magazine/1997/dom/970224/science.volcanoes.html.

▼ ***Note:*** MLA style calls for page numbers for online newspapers, magazines, and journal articles, but most online sources do not have page numbers. In such cases, insert "n. pag." for "no pagination."

Online Article from a Journal or Newsletter That Has a Print Version

After a journal's or newsletter's title, include the following print publication information: Volume number.issue number (Date): pages.

"Sugar and Hyperactivity: Is There a Connection?" Digestive Health & Nutrition 1.3 (Jan. 1997): n. pag. Online. World Wide Web. 20 Feb. 1997. Available http://www.med.harvard.edu/publications/Health_Publications/Digestive/Jan_1997/dhn197art.html.

Online Articles from a Newspaper That Has a Print Version

After a newspaper's title, include the following print publication information: [City of Publication, if not part of newspaper title] Date, edition (if any): section and pages.

Van Gelder, Lawrence. "The Grass Harp." Rev. of The Grass Harp, dir. Charles Matthau. New York Times 11 Oct. 1996: n. pag. Online. World Wide Web. 20 Feb. 1997. Available http://search.nytimes.com/web/docsroot/library/filmarchive/harp-film-review.html.

▼ ***Note:*** According to MLA style, if the article is a review, follow the title of the review with *Rev. of* [Title of Work], *by* [Author's Name] or *dir.* [Director's Name].

Internet Sources That Have No Print Versions

Note that, in MLA style, the electronic address is optional but highly recommended.

Author's Last Name, First Name. "Title of Document, Article, or Web Page." Title of Web Site or Database volume.issue number (Document Date) [or *n. d.* for "no date"]: pages or paragraphs [or *n. pag.*—for "no pagination"]. Publication Medium [use the word *Online*]. Name of Computer Network. Date Information Was Accessed. electronic address, preceded by the word *Available.*

▼ ***Note:*** If an electronic address breaks onto a second line, divide the address immediately before one of the punctuation marks within it. Do not use a hyphen or any other mark of punctuation to divide the address.

Online Reference Work That Has No Print Version

Kjeilen, Tore. "Tunisia." Encyclopaedia of the Orient. (1996): n. pag. Online. World Wide Web. 20 Feb. 1997. Available http://i-cias.com/e.o/index.htm.

Online Electronic Journal or Newsletter That Has No Print Version

Arora, Shirley L. "Proverbs in Mexican American Tradition." De Proverbio: An Electronic Journal of International Proverb Studies 1.2 (1995): n. pag. Online. World Wide Web. 20 Feb. 1997. Available http://info.utas.edu.au/docs/flonta/DP,1,2,95/MEXICAN_AMERICAN_PROVERBS.html.

World Wide Web Sites/Web Pages

Barrio, José Félix. "Ethnic Minorities." Sí, Spain (n. d.): n. pag. Online. World Wide Web. 20 Feb. 1997. Available://www.DocuWeb.ca/SiSpain/english/populati/ethnic.html.

"A Brief History of the Roma." The Patrin (10 Feb. 1997): n. pag. Online. World Wide Web. 6 February 1997. Available http://www.geocities.com/Paris/5121 /history.htm.

APA Style for Documenting Internet Sources in the Works Cited List

Unlike the MLA style, the APA style for documenting sources does not make a major distinction between sources that do have a print equivalent and sources that don't. There are several other important differences to note between MLA style and APA style for documenting sources in the Works Cited list. While MLA style calls for a hanging indent on the Works Cited entries, the APA calls for the first line of the entry to be indented. Also, MLA style requires the inclusion of the date of access for online sources; APA style does not require the date of access unless no other document date is provided. However, we recommend that the date of access be included in all cases. Finally, the APA's conventions for capitalization of titles are very different from the MLA's, as the following examples illustrate.

Online Novel, Play, or Other Entire Work

Author's Last Name, Initials (Publication Date). Title of work [Publication Medium (use the word *Online*)]. electronic address, preceded by the word *Available:* [Date Information Was Accessed].

Christie, A. (1920/1996). The mysterious affair at Styles. [Online]. Available: http://www.columbia.edu/acis/bartleby/christie/ [1997, March 6].

▼ ***Note:*** APA style allows you to indicate when a work that was originally printed has been republished online: Place the original publication date and the online publication date together in parentheses, separated by a slash.

Part of a Work

Author's Last Name, Initials (Publication Date). Name of chapter, article, or Web page. In Name of Online reference or Web site [Online]. online address, preceded by the word *Available:* [Date Information Was Accessed].

Article from an Online Reference

Kjeilen, T. (1996). Tunisia. In Encyclopaedia of the Orient [Online]. Available: http://i-cias.com/e.o/index.htm [1997, February 20].

Romany language. (1996). In Britannica online [Online]. Available: http://www.eb.com:180/ [1997, February 20].

Page from a Web Site

Barrio, J. F. (n. d.). Ethnic minorities. In Sí, Spain [Online], 6 paragraphs. Available: http://www.DocuWeb.ca/SiSpain/english/populati/ethnic.html [1997, February 20].

A brief history of the Roma. (1997). In The Patrin [Online], 10 paragraphs. Available: http://www.geocities.com/Paris/5121/history.htm [1997, February 6].

▼ ***Note:*** According to APA style, when no author is provided, begin the entry with the title of the chapter, article, or Web page, followed by the publication date. If no publication date is provided, write *n. d.* for "no date."

Article from an Online Periodical

Author's Last Name, Initials. (Publication Date). Title of article. Name of Periodical [Online], Volume Number (Issue Number) [for magazines, journals, and newsletters], Page and Section Number or Number of Paragraphs. online address, preceded by the word *Available:* [Date Information Was Accessed].

Article from an Online Journal or Newsletter

After the designation Online, include the following publication information: volume number (issue number), page number(s) or number of paragraphs in the article.

Arora, S. L. (1995). Proverbs in Mexican American tradition. De Proverbio: An Electronic Journal of International Proverb Studies [Online], 1 (2), 39 paragraphs. Available: http://info.utas.edu.au/docs/flonta/DP,1,2,95/MEXICAN_AMERICAN_PROVERBS.html [1997, February 20].

Sugar and hyperactivity: Is there a connection? (1997, January). Digestive Health & Nutrition [Online], 1 (3), 8 paragraphs. Available: http://www.med.harvard.edu/publications/Health_Publications/Digestive/Jan_1997/dhn197art.html [1997, February 20].

Article from an Online Magazine or Newspaper

Provide the month and day of publication as well as the year. After the designation *Online,* give the volume and issue number (for magazines only), then give page and section number or number of paragraphs in the article.

Kluger, J. (1997, February 24). Volcanoes with an attitude. Time [Online], 149 (8), 25 paragraphs. Available: http://pathfinder.com/time/magazine/1997/dom/970224/science.volcanoes.html [1997, February 20].

Van Gelder, L. (1997, October 11). The grass harp [Review of the film The grass harp]. New York Times [Online], 9 paragraphs. Available: http://search.nytimes.com/web/docsroot/library/filmarchive/harp-film-review.html [1997, February 20].

▼ ***Note:*** According to APA style, if the article is a review, place that information in brackets, along with the title of the work reviewed.

Style for Documenting E-Mail and Postings to Newsgroups and Forums

Because e-mail and postings to newsgroups and online forums are often not recoverable, some style manuals suggest omitting them from the Works Cited list. (The APA classifies e-mail messages and "messages from electronic bulletin boards" as "personal communications" that should be cited in text only.) However, if a student finds its necessary or desirable to include a Works Cited entry for such a source, we recommend the following formats, adapted from the MLA and APA style manuals.

Personal E-Mail Message

MLA Style:

Sender's Last Name, First Name. "Subject or Title of Message." Recipient, preceded by the words *E-mail to.* Date of Message.

Smith, Jane. "About Romani Culture." E-mail to John Doe. 27 Feb. 1997.

APA Style:

Sender's Last Name, Initials. (Year, Date of message). Subject or title of message. Recipient, preceded by the words *E-mail to.*

Smith, J. (1997, February 27). About Romani culture. E-mail to J. Doe.

Public E-Mail Message to an Online Mailing List

MLA Style:

Author's Last Name, First Name. "Subject or Title of Message." Date of Message. Name of Electronic Mailing List. Publication type (use the words *Online mailing list*). Date Message Was Accessed. address of discussion list archive (if available), preceded by the word *Available.*

Eborn, Chris. "Flamenco Dance Structure." 9 Oct. 96. Flamenco. Online mailing list. 23 Feb. 1997. Available ftp://ftp.std.com/nonprofits/dance/flamenco/d9610w41.digest.

APA Style:

Author's Last Name, Initials. (Message date). Subject of message. Name of Electronic Mailing List. [Type of medium (use the words *Online mailing list*)]. address of discussion list archive (if available), preceded by the word *Available* and a colon. [Date Message Was Accessed].

Eborn, C. (1996, October 9). Flamenco dance structure. Flamenco. Online mailing list. Available: ftp://ftp.std.com/nonprofits/dance/flamenco/d9610w41.digest. [February 23, 1997].

Posting to an Online Newgroup or Forum

MLA Style:

Author's Last Name, First Name. "Subject or Title of Posting." Date of Posting. Publication type [use the words *Online posting*]. Name or Address of Newsgroup or Forum. Online Service or Network. Date Information Was Accessed.

Karin, Cynthia. "Gypsies and/or Romany." 16 Feb. 1997. Online posting. soc.history.ancient. Usenet. 20 Feb. 1997.

APA Style:

Author's Last Name, Initials (Year, Date of Posting). Subject or title of posting. Name or address of newsgroup or forum. Online service or network. [Type of medium (use the words *Online posting*)]. [Date Information Was Accessed].

Karin, C. (1997, February 16). Gypsies and/or Romany. soc.history.ancient. Usenet. [Online posting]. [1997, February 20].

▼ ***Note:*** Students should be very selective in citing e-mail messages or public postings to newsgroups and forums. Many educational Web sites offer "ask-an-expert" services that enable students to e-mail questions to experts in various fields; in general, an e-mail response from such an expert can be considered authoritative. However, students should not assume that all e-mail correspondence is reliable, or that contributors to newsgroups and online forums are experts.

WEB RESEARCH ESSENTIALS 7

A Quick Reference to MLA Documentation Style for Internet Sources

Christie, Agatha.	**PROVIDE AUTHOR (IF ANY)**	Barrio, José Félix.
The Mysterious Affair at Styles. London: Bodley Head, 1920.	**Internet Source with a Print Equivalent** Include available print publication information. Follow your teacher's guidelines for standard documentation of print publications.	
	Internet Source with No Print Equivalent Include title of article or page; title of Internet source; volume and issue numbers, if included; publication date and page number, if included.	"Ethnic Minorities." Sí, Spain. (n. d.): n. pag. [*n. d.* stands for "no date"; *n. pag.* stands for "no pagination".]
Online.	Indicate that the document is an online source.	Online.
Bartleby Library.	**Internet Source with Print Equivalent** Provide name of Internet archive or database, if different from print publication.	
Internet.	Indicate network. (This will usually be World Wide Web; however, through the Web you can retrieve documents from archives—such as gopher sites and ftp sites—outside of the Web. In that case, simply indicate Internet.)	World Wide Web.
6 Mar. 1997.	Provide date information was accessed.	20 Feb. 1997.
Available http:// www.columbia.edu/acis /bartleby/christie	Tell where site is available (that is, provide the URL).	Available http://www.DocuWeb.c /SiSpain/english/populati/ethnic.html.
Christie, Agatha. The Mysterious Affair at Styles. London: Bodley Head, 1920. Online. Bartleby Library. Internet. 6 Mar. 1997. Available http://www.columbia .edu/acis/bartleby/christie.	Put it all together!	Barrio, José Félix. "Ethnic Minorities." Sí, Spain. (n. d.): n. pag. Online. World Wide Web. 20 Feb. 1997. Available http://www .DocuWeb.c/SiSpain/english/populati /ethnic.html.

WEB RESEARCH ESSENTIALS 8

A Quick Reference to APA Documentation Style for Internet Sources

Nonperiodical example	Element	Periodical example
Kjeilen, T. (1996).	**PROVIDE AUTHOR, IF ANY, AND PUBLICATION DATE(S), IF ANY**	Arora, S. L. (1995).
Tunisia. In <u>Encyclopaedia of the Orient</u>	**<u>Part of a Work (Nonperiodical)</u>** Provide title of work.	
	<u>Article from an Online Periodical</u> Include title of article; title of periodical.	Proverbs in Mexican American tradition. <u>De Proverbio: An Electronic Journal of International Proverb Studies</u>
[Online].	Indicate that the document is an online source.	[Online],
	<u>Article from an Online Periodical</u> Provide volume number and issue number (except for newspaper articles); provide number of paragraphs in article.	<u>1</u> (2), 39 paragraphs.
Available: http://i-cias.com/e.o./index.htm	Tell where the source is available (that is, provide the URL).	Available: http://info.utas.edu.au/docs/flonta/DP,1,2,95/MEXICAN_AMERICAN_PROVERBS.html
[1997, February 18].	Provide date information was accessed.	[1997, February 20].
Kjeilen. T. (1996). Tunisia. In <u>Encyclopaedia of the Orient</u> [Online]. Available: http://i-cias.com/e.o./index.htm [1997, February 18].	Put it all together!	Arora, S. L. (1995). Proverbs in Mexican American tradition. <u>De Proverbio: An Electronic Journal of International Proverb Studies</u> [Online], <u>1</u> (2), 39 paragraphs. Available: http://info.utas.edu.au/docs/flonta/DP,1,2,95/MEXICAN_AMERICAN_PROVERBS.html [1997, February 20].

NAME ______________________ CLASS ________________ DATE ____________

ACTIVITY 5 Web Source Log

Worksheet

Name of Web Page: ______________________

Name of Web Site or Archive: ______________________

Print Information, if any: ______________________

Name of Book Publisher: ______________________

Volume and Issue/Edition: ______________________

Date of Book's Publication: ______________________

Date of Web Site's Publication: ______________________

Date of Access: ______________________

URL: ______________________

Comments: ______________________

Name of Web Page: ______________________

Name of Web Site or Archive: ______________________

Print Information, if any: ______________________

Name of Book Publisher: ______________________

Volume and Issue/Edition: ______________________

Date of Book's Publication: ______________________

Date of Web Site's Publication: ______________________

Date of Access: ______________________

URL: ______________________

Comments: ______________________

APPENDIX B: WORLD WIDE WEB RESOURCES

News and Information

The Washington Post

http://www.washingtonpost.com/
Daily news from *The Washington Post,* as well as compilations of related stories from the past months.

The Boston Globe

http://www.boston.com/
Similar information to that in any newspaper Web site, but more user-friendly than most.

Yahooligans

http://www.yahooligans.com/
An index of kids' Web sites on the Internet. Like the Yahoo directory <www.yahoo.com>, this page gives established categories for searching the Net and allows customized searches too. The results are a list of home pages of general interest to children on a desired subject.

Resources

Project Gutenberg

http://www.promo.net/pg/
Started in 1971 with a $100 million grant from the University of Illinois, Project Gutenberg is an enormous searchable database of literature and reference works stored in libraries around the country. Read complete texts online or research single answers.

Book Stacks Unlimited

http://www.books.com/scripts/lib.exe
Read text manuscripts online.

References

The World Lecture Hall

http://www.utexas.edu/world/lecture
Course syllabi, assignments, lecture notes, exams, class calendars, and more for various subjects are available in this virtual environment.

Kathy Shrock's Guide for Educators

http://www.capecod.net/Wixon/
Education projects from creative writing ideas to practical applications such as description, making an almanac, and producing a class newspaper. Projects are divided and identified by grade level appropriateness. Includes projects for Vocational Education, Science, and Math.

Educational Launch Pad

http://serv2.fwi.com/~woliver/Educational_LAUNCH_PAD.html
Many links to educational sites including museums, libraries, and dictionaries. Also links to many resources for educators.

The Virtual Schoolhouse

http://sunsite.unc.edu/cisco/schoolhouse.html
Links to educational sites all over the world. Virtual libraries and classrooms link to real ones that can provide homework help on specific subjects. Includes areas just for educators.

CIA World Factbook

http://www.odci.gov/cia/publications/nsolo/wfb-all.htm
Geography and social studies information on every country in the world. Includes location, type of government, population, and downloadable maps.

The Virtual Reference Desk

http://thorplus.lib.purdue.edu/reference/index.html
Every type of reference material you can imagine.

The Busy Teacher's Web Site

http://www.ceismc.gatech.edu/BusyT/
Comprehensive source for materials, lesson plans, and classroom activities organized by subject area. Includes references and searchable databases.

Library of Congress

http://lcweb.loc.gov/homepage/lchp.html
Government information and historical exhibits are available on this Web site, as well as information on a vast number of books and publications.

The White House

http://www.whitehouse.gov/WH
Take a virtual tour, discover the history of the building, read about the First Families, then find out in the Briefing Room what's going on in the White House today.

College Board Online

http://www.collegeboard.org
Register for SATs, get information on attending prospective colleges and universities all over the world, and find out about financial aid for higher education.

Educational Testing Service

http://www.ets.org
A Web site from ETS with research information on careers and job search sites, practice test question for all ETS tests including SAT, GMAT, GRE, and TOEFL. Students can also register for tests online.

Cornell University Legal Information Institute

http://www.law.cornell.edu/lii.table.html
Full text documents including the U.S. Constitution and other important federal papers, recent and historic Supreme Court decisions, and links to law libraries and resource lists.

Ask an Expert

http://www.askanexpert.com/askanexpert
Ask a question by e-mail on just about any subject, and have experts in the field look up an answer for you.

Teaching Critical Evaluation Skills for World Wide Web Resources

http://www.widener.edu/libraries.html/
Access this site by selecting the link "Evaluating Web Resources" at the URL above.

Science

The Discovery Channel Online

http://www.discovery.com/

The online version of the popular cable television channel. Lots of information on science topics of interest to students. Links to other science-related pages.

Today at NASA

http://www.hq.nasa.gov/office/pao/NewsRoom/today.html

Links to all the NASA sites including their page on the Space Shuttle with realtime data and pictures from the shuttle. Also has links to news stories on what's going on in outer space today. Updated daily.

Quest-NASA Interactive

http://quest.arc.nasa.gov/

Interactive NASA projects for school-age students. Projects include *Live from Mars,* in which students travel (virtually) along with the two NASA spacecraft currently exploring the planet Mars.

Bill Nye, the Science Guy

http://nyelabs.kcts.org/

The online pages of the popular television show host who makes science understandable to just about everyone. This page has links to several outstanding science sites, including the Field Museum of Natural History in Chicago and the Smithsonian Institution in Washington, D.C. It also features a virtual tour of the solar system and a virtual frog dissection online.

The Why Files

http://whyfiles.news.wisc.edu

The science behind the news—a supplement to current events curriculum.

Environmental Protection Agency

http://www.epa.gov/

Resources, regulations, publications, teaching aids/curriculum guides on everything from ecosystems to trash, facts about environmental problems ranging from acid rain to pesticides, and links to other environmental education sites.

Bat Conservation International

http://www.batcon.org/

Learn all about bats and why they are important to the environment. Factual information and links to fun and informative sites. Activities for educators at all grade levels.

National Institutes of Health

http://www.nih.gov/

Information on and links to health information, biomedical data, scientific resources, activities, grant information, and access to the NIH Library.

National Library of Medicine

http://www.nlm.nih.gov/

Information on health and medical topics. Links and databases and special information programs, publications, and research projects.

Language Arts

Inkspot, Resources for Young Writers

http://www.interlog.com/~ohi/inkspot/young.html
Research, plan, and publish online.

The Children's Literature Web Guide

http://www.ucalgary.ca/~dkbrown/index.html
Internet resources related to books for children and young adults. Includes book reviews and teaching ideas for educators.

The Complete Works of William Shakespeare

http://the-tech.mit.edu/Shakespeare.html
Complete text of all of Shakespeare's plays with hypertext links to a glossary and other Shakespeare sites online.

Social Studies/Geography

PCL Map Collection

http://www.lib.utexas.edu/Libs/PCL/Map_collection/National_parks/National_parks.html
Over 230,000 maps to choose from, topographical and political, of places all over the world.

City.Net

http://www.city.net
Information on cities and countries throughout the world—including maps, statistics, historical facts, local media lists, and many other resources.

Weather

The Weather Channel

http://www.weather.com
Online version of cable television's weather channel. Includes local forecasts and maps, satellite images, weather data, links to related weather sites.

Weather Net

http://cirrus.sprl.umich.edu/wxnet/
Another weather site with forecasts, maps, historical weather data, links to related weather sites.

Special Education

Internet Resources for Special Education

http://www.interactive.net/~wader/sped.htm
Special Education resources for educators and their students. Technical information and classroom resources include classroom projects for the Internet. Lots of information and links to other places. More user-friendly than sites with similar information.

Special Education Resources on the Internet

http://www.hood.edu/seri/serihome.htm
Massive listing of worldwide Special Education resources, mostly factual information on individual disorders or syndromes; medical references and case histories; and links to university studies, clearinghouses, journal articles, and discussion groups.

Math

Ask Dr. Math

http://forum.swarthmore.edu/dr.math
A virtual center for math education on the Internet. Funded by the National Science Foundation. Ask specific questions or research math-related topics online.

Foreign Languages

ZIA Education Languages Page

http://www.zia.com/educate/language/default.htm
Links to sites for actively learning languages. Also links to many other valuable sites for all educators.

National K-12 Foreign Language Resource Center at Iowa State University

http://www.educ.iastate.edu/currinst/nflrc/nflrc.html
Many great links to educational resources and foreign-language sites on the World Wide Web. Includes lists of foreign-language e-mail pen pals and cross-curriculum projects.

Nerd World-Education-Languages

http://www.nerdworld.com/nw1306.html
Links to a huge variety of resources for foreign language educators and others interested in world languages including Latin, Arabic, Gaelic, Indonesian, Japanese, and many more.

Selected Search Engines and Directories

AltaVista

http://www.altavista.digital.com

Excite

http://www.excite.com/

HotBot

http://www.hotbot.com

Infoseek

http://www.infoseek.com/

Lycos

http://www.lycos.com

WebCrawler

http://www.webcrawler.com

Yahoo

http://www.yahoo.com

Web Sources Cited in the Video

Visualization Study of the NSFNET
http://www.ncsa.uiuc.edu/SCMS/DigLib/text/technology/Visualization-Study-NSFNET-Cox.html

Netscape's Net Search Page
http://home.netscape.com/home/internet-search.html

University of Michigan Documents Center: Foreign Government/Country Background Information
http://www.lib.umich.edu/libhome/Documents.center/forcoun.html

Library of Congress Country Studies
http://lcweb2.loc.gov/frd/cs/cshome.html

Sí, Spain
http://www.docuweb.ca./SiSpain/index.html

Britannica Online
http://www.eb.com:180

Romani Rights Web
http://hamp.hampshire.edu/~ratS88/romani

The Patrin
http://www.geocities.com/Paris/5121/patrin.htm

GLOSSARY: INTERNET AND WORLD WIDE WEB TERMS

browser or Web browser A **client** software program that enables you to search for and view **Web pages.** Netscape Navigator and Microsoft Internet Explorer are two examples.

client A computer or computer software program used to retrieve files or information from a **server** (such as an Internet **host**) over a network.

country code Two-letter abbreviations at the end of some **hostnames** that identify the countries in which a **server** is located. For example, the hostname for Yahoo's server in Japan, *www.yahoo.co.jp,* ends with *jp,* the country code for Japan.

cyberspace The electronic environment of computers and networks through which people communicate and share digital information—in contrast to the "real" world of face-to-face, physical, nonelectronic interaction.

directory[1] Parts of a **path,** separated by slashes, that precede a **filename.** For example, Yahoo's **Web site** contains a page titled "Yahoo! Information." Its **URL,** <http://www.yahoo.com/docs/info/index.html>, shows that the page (whose filename is *index.html*) is stored in the directory *info,* which is stored in the directory *docs,* which is stored in the main (unnamed) directory of the **server** *www.yahoo.com.*

directory[2] Name for a **Web site,** such as Yahoo <http://www.yahoo.com>, that indexes individual **Web pages** using multilevel browsable categories or "subject trees" based on the information the pages contain. The highest level of Yahoo, for example, contains very broad category headings such as *Arts, News,* and *Entertainment.* The Arts category contains subcategories such as *Architecture, Humanities,* and *Performing Arts.* The categories become progressively more specific until they reach a level such as *Arts: Humanities: Literature: Genres: Poetry: Poets,* which contains a **hypertext** list of Web pages about specific poets across the ages.

domains Parts of a **hostname** that identify the levels of Internet hierarchy to which a **host** belongs. For example, *lcweb.loc.gov* is the hostname for a computer labeled *lcweb* that is in the *loc* (Library of Congress) domain, which is in the top-level domain *gov,* because the Library of Congress is a part of the federal government. Other top-level domains include *com, edu, mil, org,* and *net.* **Country codes** are sometimes used in place of top-level domains.

DNS Domain Name System. System that translates **hostnames,** such as *home.netscape.com,* into corresponding numerical addresses that computers can understand.

file Document, image, sound, program, or other item stored within a **directory**[1] on a computer.

filename Name assigned to a **file** stored on a computer. Files stored on the same **server** may have the same name as long as they do not have the same **path.** Yahoo's **home page** <http://www.yahoo.com/index.html> and its "Yahoo information" page <http://www.yahoo.com/docs/info/index.html> have the same filename *(index.html),* but different paths.

filename extension Abbreviation at the end of the **filename** that indicates what type of **file** it is. Extensions used on the Internet include *.html* or *.htm* for **Web pages** and *.gif* and *.jpg* for graphic files.

form Section of a **Web page** where you can type in information to send to a **server.** For example, every Web **search engine** provides a form that has at least one field or window where you can type in keywords, and at least one "button" (often labeled *Search*) that tells your Web **browser** to send the keywords to the search engine's server. After the server processes your request, it returns the resulting information to you.

FTP File Transfer Protocol. The protocol most often used to transfer large **files,** such as electronic books, over the Internet.

gopher Menu-based information retrieval protocol that predates the **World Wide Web.** Although gopher servers are still in use, most people will find it easier to use Web **search engine** sites to look for information on the Internet.

home page Commonly, the first **Web page** you will see when accessing a **server** or **Web site.** Home pages usually serve as gateways or starting points from which you may follow **hyperlinks** to other related Web pages.

host Internet **server** having a unique numerical address and, usually, a **hostname.** With the right **client** software, such as a Web **browser,** you can connect to a host and retrieve **files** or information from it.

hostname Name of an Internet **server,** found in a **URL** just after the **protocol** code and before the **path.** In the URL <http://www.yahoo.com/docs/info/index.html>, the hostname is *www.yahoo.com* and the path is */docs/info.*

HTML Hypertext Markup Language. Coding system used to create **Web pages.** Web pages are actually plain text **files** marked up with HTML codes that tell a **browser** how the text, images, links, and other parts of the page should be styled and arranged.

HTTP Hypertext Transfer Protocol. Main **protocol** used on the **World Wide Web. URL**s that begin with *http://* are usually **Web pages.** Web **browsers** also recognize other protocols, such as **FTP** and **gopher.**

hypertext or **hyperlink** Coded text or graphics within a **Web page,** usually in a contrasting color and often underlined, that link with or point to content elsewhere on the **Web.** Following a hyperlink by clicking on it with a mouse will tell a **browser** to display the item to which it links. *Hypertext* usually refers only to text links, while *hyperlink* may refer to either text links or graphical links. Non-text links are sometimes called *hypermedia.*

path Portion of a **URL** that immediately follows the **hostname.** In the URL for the **home page** of the State Department's "Background Notes" on foreign countries <http://www.state.gov/www/background_notes/index.html>, the complete path for the **file** *index.html* is */www/background_notes/*. Paths tell computers to look for files within certain **directories**[1]; in this case, the *background_notes* subdirectory of the www directory of the server *www.state.gov.*

protocol Established set of rules for transferring signals and information among computers, printers, modems, and other machines. Internet protocols include **FTP, HTTP, gopher,** and **telnet.**

search engine Tool at certain **Web sites** (such as *AltaVista, Excite, HotBot, Infoseek, Inktomi, Lycos, WebCrawler*) that enables you to type in keywords and search for Internet resources that contain them.

server Computer or computer software program that delivers **files** and information requested by **client** programs over a network. For example, a **Web** server can deliver **Web pages** to a personal computer that is running a **browser** program.

telnet **Protocol** that allows you to log onto a remote computer. Unlike the **Web,** telnet is capable of displaying plain text only, but no **hyperlinks** or multimedia.

URL Uniform Resource Locator. Complete address for a **file** that can be accessed over the Internet. A URL starts with a code describing the **protocol** needed to retrieve the file (*http://* for **Web pages,** *ftp://* for **FTP files,** and so on), continues with the **hostname,** then the **path,** then the **filename.** For example, the URL for the "Net Search" page maintained by Netscape is <http://home.netscape.com/home/internet-search.html>.

Usenet Collection of online discussion groups or bulletin boards, called *newsgroups,* that can be accessed over the Internet.

Web or **World Wide Web** The part of the Internet where you can publish and access multimedia-enriched **Web pages.**

Web page Document on the **World Wide Web,** coded in **HTML,** that has a unique **URL.** There is no limit to how long a particular Web page may be—it might be a document that fills up only half a screen, or it might be one that would fill a hundred 8 1/2 by 11-inch pages if printed out. Web pages may contain pictures, sounds, animation, and video in addition to styled text.

Web site Collection of related **Web pages,** connected by **hyperlinks,** and stored in a **directory**[1] or set of directories within the same **server.** For example, the State Department server *dosweb.lib.uic.edu* contains the Web site for the Department's "Background Notes" on numerous foreign countries. It can be accessed through the State Department's home page or at the URL <http://www.state.gov/www/background_notes/index.html>. The page provides hyperlinks that, when followed, will lead you through the site to Web pages consisting of full text reports on individual countries. An Internet server may contain just one site, or many.

ANSWER KEYS

Worksheet 1: K-W-L-W-L
(page 6)

Responses, especially in columns 3, 4, and 5, should reveal that students have actively viewed the video and have carefully considered its subject matter.

Worksheet 2: Using a Browser
(page 16)

Part One: For the correct labels, see the Web Research Essentials 2 handout.

Part Two:

1. Toolbar Buttons (general description): Click these to activate some of the most commonly-used navigation commands. (For descriptions of individual buttons, see the Web Research Essentials 2 handout.)
2. Menus (general description): Select commands from these, including all of the commands on the Toolbar. (For descriptions of the *File* and *Bookmarks/Favorites* menus, see the Web Research Essentials 2 handout.)
3. Directory Buttons: Click these to get to predetermined Web pages.
4. Title Bar: Shows the title of the page currently displayed.
5. Location Window: Shows the URL of the page currently displayed.
6. Main Window: Displays the page at the URL in the Location Window.
7. Status Line: Shows the URL for any hyperlink to which the cursor is pointing; gives other information when you connect to a server; tells how much of a page has loaded and how fast a page is loading.
8. Progress Bar: Graphically represents how much of a total page has loaded.
9. Scrollbar and Scroll Buttons: Use to move up and down through pages.

Worksheet 3: Searching the Web
(page 24)

Part One: Compare students' keyword choices to their subject descriptions, and suggest keywords that they may not have considered. Assess how well students were able to refine their searches, and indicate refinements (Boolean operators, symbols, or quotation marks) that might have made the searches more successful. Using a Web browser, view at least some of the pages students found. Select a few to present to the class as models of useful sources that were found through well-constructed searches.

Part Two: Compare students' category choices to their subject descriptions in Part One, and suggest alternate categories that they may not have considered. View at least some of the pages students found, and select a few to present to the class as models of useful sources that were found through effective use of a Web directory.

Part Three: View at least some of the page students found, and select a few to present as models of sources that might be helpful in narrowing a subject.

Note any recurring problems that students had while completing the assignment. Discuss the problems and possible solutions with the class.

Worksheet 4: Evaluating Web Sources (page 33)

Responses should reveal an knowledge of the evaluation criteria in the handout Web Research Essentials 5, and the types of sites listed in the handout Web Research Essentials 6. Questions are matched with appropriate criteria below.

Question Number	Criteria
1 and 2	Coverage
3	Currency
4, 5, 6 and 11	Authority
7 and 8	Accuracy
9, 10, 11, 12, 13	Objectivity, types of sites
14	(overall evaluation)

Reteach criteria with which students had difficulty. View at least some of the pages students evaluated; present a few to the class as models of useful online sources.